A SIGNALLER'S WAR
Notes Compiled from My Diary 1914-1918

Sgt. Bernard Brookes

Published by Una Barrie.

© 2012 Sgt. Bernard Brookes. All rights reserved.
ISBN 978-1-471-77890-2

CONTENTS

Table of Figures v

About this Book ix

Foreword xi

Notes Compiled from My Diary 1
    Preface 3
    Introduction 5
    Chapter 1 7
    Chapter 2 21
    Chapter 3 57
    Chapter 4 111
    Chapter 5 157
    Chapter 6 159
    Epilogue 173
    Conclusion 177

Appendix 179

TABLE OF FIGURES

1. Diary and Notebooks viii
2. Open Diary and Notebooks viii
3. Notes Compiled from My Diary 1
4. Sgt. Bernard Brookes 1893-1962 2
5. New Recruits 10
6. Soldiers at Rest 15
7. Last Letter from England 20
8. First Letter from France 24
9. Armentières 34
10. Queen's Westminster Battalion Casualties 35
11. Erquinghem Station 38
12. Cartoon 42
13. Princess Mary Christmas Card 1914 51
14. King and Queen Christmas Card 1914 52
15. German Signatures 53
16. Sketch of Trenches at Houplines 58
17. Three DCMs for QWR 63
18. Map of Ypres 66
19. Chateau de la Rose, Houplines 68
20. Alice, a boy and Suzanne 70
21. Some Diet! 73
22. Shell Near Allies' Trenches 83
23. Author in Chateau Grounds 87
24. Signal 89
25. Houplines Church after First Shelling 90
26. Sketch of Position of Church and Chateau at Houplines 94
27. Wrecking of a Church 96
28. Chateau de la Rose, Houplines after Bombing 101
29. Cloth Hall 1913 106
30. Cloth Hall after Bombing 109
31. Short Street of Ypres after Bombing 110
32. In the Heart of Ypres after Bombing 110

33. Report from an Irish Soldier 141
34. Sketch of Position of Stink Cottages 142
35. Sketch of Author 148
36. Wounded British Soldiers 156
37. Lord Loreburn 159
38. St Anselm's 160
39. Letter Home 160
40. Neurasthenia Report 161
41. Sports' Day 162
42. St Anselm's Reception Room 163
43. Letter from Convalescence 164
44. Patients in St Anselm's 165
45. St Anselm's Hospital Grace 165
46. St Anselm's Hospital Alphabet 166
47. Retreat House for Men 171
48. The First Retreat for Catholic Soldiers 171
49. Nurses' Signatures 174
50. The Monthly Tonic 176
51. King George V with Author in Attendance 177
52. The King and Queen Visit Hospitals at Epsom 178
53. "Queen's" Memorial Window, Westminster Abbey 180
54. Prince of Wales Unveils Memorial 180
55. Home Guard 1945 181
56. Author with Nora and Family, VE day 1945 181
57. Trenches, Sanctuary Wood 2004 182
58. Shell Holes, Sanctuary Wood 2004 182

1. Diary and Notebooks

2. Open Diary and Notebooks

About this Book

At the outbreak of WWI, my father, Bernard Brookes, then aged 21, joined the Queen's Westminster Rifles. He kept a record of his experiences in notebooks and later typed these up into a diary along with letters, postcards and other items that he collected during his time on the frontline. After demobilisation, he worked for the Société Générale bank (using the French he had learnt in the trenches). He married Nora Cole in 1919; they went on to have five children and 17 grandchildren. In WWII, he joined the Home Guard. He died in 1962.

I should like to thank all those who helped me in the preparation of my father's diary for publication: my daughter, Jackie Barrie, for the cover design and her invaluable advice and encouragement without which I could not have got started; my daughter, Rosemary Godfrey, for formatting the manuscript; my daughter, Frances Rogers for the painting of poppy fields used for the cover; my husband, John, for proofreading it; my son-in-law, Paul Godfrey, for scanning all the images; and my nephew, Robert Brookes, who was responsible for copying the original document into Word.

This version of the diary comprises the complete text with a selection of images. We have endeavoured to remain faithful to the original script but have added some later events in my father's life and other photos to bring it up-to-date. The footnotes reproduce annotations pencilled by my father in 1939.

In 1984, the diary was bound in leather and exhibited at the Imperial War Museum. It has also been lent to the BBC, while the section on the Christmas Truce was quoted in the magazine, "Britain at War" (see pages 48-53). In 2009, the page of German signatures was auctioned by Bonhams for £1,080, but we have no record of when it became separated from the rest of the documents and its present whereabouts is unknown.

The original diary and notebooks are in the keeping of Brookes family members. There are also versions online, including scans of all the original pages (text and images). To find them, please do an Internet search for "Bernard Brookes war diary".

All proceeds from the sale of the book are being donated to the Royal British Legion, to help those brave men and women who have been wounded in the service of their country.

This book is dedicated to my father's memory.

Una Barrie,
Author's Daughter

July 2012

Foreword

Bernard Brookes' first-hand account of life in the trenches on the Western Front in 1914-15 is particularly graphic. You really feel that you are there alongside him.

From the earliest days of the war until he was invalided home in the summer of 1915, he served on, or close to, the front line in Flanders' fields and kept a diary on which this book is based. As a Signaller whose duty required him to run to the forward platoons with messages, his job was among the most dangerous. He describes what he saw and heard around him over that period – the experience of living in water-filled trenches, the intense cold, the shelling, the gas attacks, the death of 'chums' standing next to him. But he also describes the lighter side of service on the Western Front – exchanging souvenirs with German soldiers in the Christmas Truce, nights when the Germans would entertain both sides singing well-known British songs played on a bugle, periods away from the front line, visits to French 'estaminets'. And his account is well illustrated by postcards, photographs, sketches and handwritten letters from his scrapbook.

The result is a book which has much relevance and interest, particularly for those who, a hundred years on, want to know what it was actually like for a young soldier to serve in the trenches of the First World War.

I am most grateful to Bernard's family for so generously donating to the Royal British Legion all proceeds from the book. The Legion was founded shortly after the First World War to support all those who had fought in that conflict and their families. It is now supporting a younger generation whose experiences of war are of very different conflicts, such as those in Iraq and Afghanistan. Bernard Brookes was only twenty two when he returned from his war – much the same age as many are leaving the

British Army today – and reading his book, it struck me that although he and this younger generation are separated from each other by many years, they are remarkably close to each other in spirit.

Lieutenant General Sir John Kiszely KCB MC,
National President, The Royal British Legion

August 2012

NOTES COMPILED FROM MY DIARY

NOTES COMPILED FROM MY DIARY.

A True Personal Record of Experiences as a

Signaller in the Army, at Home and Abroad during

THE EUROPEAN WAR. (1914).

written by

Sergeant Bernard Joseph Brookes,

1/16 Battalion County of London Regiment,

(Queen's Westminster Rifles).

3. Notes Compiled from My Diary

4. Sgt. Bernard Brookes 1893-1962

Preface

Whoever may read these notes must not expect a record of gallant deeds, but a true indication of the conditions and life in the Army with its sorrows and joys, monotony and fun, work and play both at home and overseas, which is the lot of every infantryman.

Except for the reasons of indicating the style of work and duty, to say nothing of the hardships, I have left out anything which I have had personally to do or put up with if it is at all out of the ordinary, but I have only penned such things that might, and do, continually happen to any infantryman in the British Army.

There are many points mentioned herein which perhaps may not be of the slightest interest to any but myself, but it must be remembered that my chief object in writing my experiences whilst serving as a soldier in this "War" is to have a record for reference in future years and to call to mind any incidents which might otherwise be forgotten.

To others who read these pages, the continual repetition of various incidents may prove monotonous, but life in the Army, either at Home or Overseas is itself monotonous.

It should also be remembered that the hardships and privations which may be mentioned are daily occurrences and not special to the writer.

BERNARD JOSEPH BROOKES,
Sergeant

Orderly Room,
Convalescent Hospital,
Woodcote Park, Epsom.

31st December 1916

Introduction

28.6.1914

On Sunday 28th June in the year 1914 I was at Newport in Monmouthshire, having completed one week of a cycling tour through Gloucestershire, the Black Mountains in South Wales and the beautiful Wye Valley.

Whilst walking down the High Street, I noticed a crowd outside the local Newspaper Office and I saw the announcement of the assassination of the Archduke Francis Ferdinand of Austria and his wife, the Duchess of Hohenburg, at Sarajevo.

I continued on my way having forgotten almost as soon as I had read this announcement, like so many others, and I never imagined how far reaching the effect of this assassination would be and how our enemies would use it as an excuse to start the sanguinary War in which nearly all civilised Europe is now engaged.

But as this is a personal history, let me look at it in a personal light. It meant to me that before long I was to give up my peaceful (if somewhat dull) life in England to be placed in a short time on the Battlefield, where I, like so many of my fellow-countrymen, would have to fight an enemy who is without scruples - to live for months, knowing that any minute might be the last - with bloodshed, sickness, hunger, thirst and all the hardships which are necessarily the lot of a Soldier in such a War as is now raging on the Continent.

Chapter 1

England

From 29th June 1914 until 1st November 1914

29.6.1914

I continued on my Cycle Tour leaving Newport the next day, Monday the 29th June 1914, by boat for Ilfracombe, and then cycled on touching Lynton, Lynmouth, Porlock (where is the hill which is considered the worst in England), Bridgewater, Cheddar, Wells, Glastonbury (with its fine ruins), Stratton-on-Fosse, Frome, Salisbury and arrived back in London on Saturday the 4th July.

28.7.1914

Events moved rapidly and the War cloud looked as though it could not be dispersed and the climax was reached when on Tuesday the 28th July, between Austria and Serbia a State of War was declared. London was all excitement and before the end of the month the Bank Rate had leaped from 3% to 8%, and on the 1st August it stood at 10%.

3.8.1914

On Monday 3rd August (Bank Holiday) I went to the City in case War was declared by England and anything of importance should have to be done. Although the Firm I am with is Belgian, the Representative Principal and many in the business were Germs. Some of them had already left for Germany to fight against us, but there were still several at the Office who had not got the pluck to return and fight for their Country. As I write I am pleased to say that the Office is now clear of anything Germy, and it is resolved that none of the Germs will ever set foot in the Office again if it is possible to avoid it.

4.8.1914

An ultimatum which England presented to Germany expired at 11.00pm on Tuesday the 4th August 1914 and from that time War was the order of the day.

5.8.1914

The next day, upon representations being made to an English Principal in the Firm, a promise was made that full salary would be paid and one's position in the Firm assured at the conclusion of hostilities for those who joined the colours.

6.8.1914

I tried to join the West Kent Yeomanry but they were full up.

7.8.1914

I immediately took steps to join a regiment and on Friday 7th August 1914, with Frank Croxford and George Steptoe (two colleagues from the Office) I went to the Headquarters of the 16th Battalion of the County of London Regiment, the Queen's Westminster Rifles and after waiting outside 58, Buckingham Gate for two or three hours we struggled and pushed our way inside as soon as the door was opened - we were all so eager to join the Army. Strange to say, that men I have met since who have returned from the Front are even more eager to get out of it now, but although one had to wait a long time to get into the Army at the beginning of the War, one has to wait a sight longer to get out once in the Army.

After much swearing outside the building, we were "sworn in" and then waited in turn to see the Doctor. I passed the Doctor as "Fit" and was posted to "E" Company. We then paid our entrance fee (rather a good idea - pay to serve one's country) and the receipt for this money permitted free travelling on the Motor Omnibuses and other conveyances, although in civilian clothes. Unfortunately this practice was not continued long enough to make up the entrance fee, but I honestly did my best.[1]

8.8.1914

On Saturday 8th August I did my first drill which consisted chiefly of "marking time", "right turning" and "forming fours" in the rain, which made me wish (so soon) that I had not been quite so keen in "joining up" and had left it until after the weekend. On Sunday also we turned out for drill although we were still in civilian clothes, the necessary supply of khaki not being forthcoming.

11.8.1914

On Tuesday 11th August, Lieutenant-Colonel R. Shoolbred addressed the Battalion and asked the men to volunteer for Foreign Service. With large ideas of spending the winter in Egypt and on the whole having a rather good holiday (but not with the slightest thought of fighting or danger) we proudly agreed to serve in Foreign lands.

16.8.1914

I had been sleeping at home all this time and had no uniform, but on Sunday 16th August for the first time I slept in Westminster Schools. Of course this was my first experience of sleeping on boards, but it is not so bad on the floor when once one gets used to it.

22.8.1914

My pride reached its height when on Saturday 22nd August I got into my uniform. I did not know the correct way to adjust puttees (for there is a knack) but I got them fixed some way or another. I also wore my bayonet (which afterwards I learnt is only allowed to sergeants when off parade), and with my head high in the air went to Victoria and took the train to Epsom to meet the Cycling Club which had gone that way for their weekly ride. I slept at home that night.

25.8.1914

Tuesday 25th August saw us on our first Route March which was past Buckingham Palace and through the Park, and I am sure we

---

[1] ? date when marched to Tower of London to draw Boer War rifles (9½lbs long Lee Enfield).

were all very proud when the Guards outside the Palace "Presented Arms" to us. We were "some" soldiers.

5. New Recruits

26.8.1914

On Wednesday the 26th August we were informed that the next day was to see us on our way to a training camp and this evening we had an excellent concert (very similar to those we have since had at the Front). It is very sad to look back and think that one or two singers of note who were so gay have now paid the price and given their lives for their Country.

27.8.1914

On Thursday the 27th August there was a Requiem Mass at Westminster Cathedral for the Pope, who died on 20th August, and after various inspections I managed to drop in at the Cathedral. After dinner we paraded in the playground and with rifles at the "trail" (for a rifle regiment does not "slope arms") swung out of the gate to the echo of hearty cheering. Our hearts were full and we felt proud and happy.

The rain came on as we were marching down Victoria Street and instead of going through the City we dropped under the earth and took the tube to Euston. We had to parade outside the station and of course I forgot my place and number, for which I was called over the coals by Captain Shattock, but in the words of the song

"What did I care?" for I had my rifle and khaki and a fairly good opinion of myself as a soldier.

We took the train to Boxmoor and some of the men had their people at the station and we got a good send off.

When we arrived at Boxmoor it was very hot. We paraded outside the station (and I remembered my place this time) and had a three and a half miles march before us to Leverstock Green. By the time we had mastered the first hill (for there were several) I had lost all my pride and would willingly have given my rifle to anyone who might have liked it (and many others would have done the same), but no doubt we would have wanted them back later. What we realised was the difference between our Route March for a short distance on level ground in London and an uphill march feeling hungry and thirsty on a hot day.

We got to our quarters at about 6.00pm and "E" Company were at Well Farm. We had some tea (without milk) and were placed on real Army diet for the first time. Before we had been looked after by a caterer and on the whole we had good grub, although once some tinned fruit had upset half the Company and two men had to go to Hospital. Some "old soldiers" however put us up to the tricks of the trade and we all had pains in our "Little Marys" (not too bad mind you), but just enough to keep us off parade on a hot day, this by the way.

After looking round the barn and the farm one of the fellows asked me if I would care for a walk round and I readily consented. We returned at 9.30pm to find that various Sergeants and Corporals had been looking for us and that we should not have left our quarters without permission. Being new to Army discipline no fuss was made about the matter, but I was detailed for "Mess Orderly" for the next day. (Resolution: I must not forget that I am training for war and am not on a holiday).

I had better explain the important duties of a "Mess Orderly" which I had the honour to perform. It meant rising half-an-hour before the others, i.e. that is at 5.00am ("some shiver") to cut up the bacon for the Cook, and after meals wash up the cooking utensils. I found that what with getting up so early, working as Orderly, and parades during the day, by the time it was evening I was fairly tired. I laid my weary body on its straw bed and my coconut on my kit-bag and dropped off into a sound sleep. At 11.15pm we had a "Night Alarm" and had to turn out into the cold to see how long it would take us to get clear of our quarters in the event of such a necessity arising. As far as I remember, I created the record (though unfortunately at the wrong end), for our barn was the last out and I was the last out of the barn.

29.8.1914

The next night was a little less exciting for we were not turned out of our "beds" (straw thrown over the floor), but were not allowed in them as we had "Night Operations" from 9.00pm until 11.00pm. For the uninitiated let me explain what "Night Operations" are. According to the Army it is practising to march in the dark, silently and keeping in perfect order. Instead of having commands shouted out, one must, by constant watching, see what has to be done by noticing the movements of the men on either side and do likewise as smartly as if on the Barrack Square. As a matter of fact it actually consists of men jumping on one another's heels, much swearing and finishing up by getting hopelessly lost. However after a short time one improves and "Night Ops." are really of the utmost importance as so much work is done at night at the Front and of course noiselessness is essential.

30.8.1914

The next day being a Sunday, the Catholics paraded in undress uniform and marched to Church at Boxmoor and as it was a nice day and we had no equipment, we quite enjoyed the journey. At Church, Sergeant Major W.J. Price (who has lately been awarded the D.C.M.) came up with his men (R.F.A.) and I had a chat with him, again feeling proud (I soon lost my pride however) a Rifleman on familiar terms with a Sergeant Major. During the afternoon I called on Frank Carroll in the Civil Service Rifles at Bedmond (which by the way was out of bounds) and we had tea in a cottage.

31.8.1914

On Monday 31st August I certainly had a stroke of luck and it amounted to this, that Colour Sergeant Turnball (since awarded the D.C.M.) told me that I had been appointed a Signaller for "E" Company with Harrow and Rolfe. Why I was picked out for this duty, I really cannot say, but I believe that the Colour Sergeant must have had some bad reports about me, (for I had done any amount of things I should not) and I was seen by him yesterday at Bedmond and have come to the conclusion that he thought that as a soldier, I was likely to be a "wash out".

Well I must say that I did not take kindly to the work of an infantryman in the Company. There is plenty of dirty work to do, guards, fatigues etc. and it is very monotonous, and looking back now, I feel sure that I would have disliked it intensely in France (for as you will see I was with the Company for a period at the Front) and feel sure that I could never have "stuck it", but I took a liking to Signalling, found it very interesting and not at all monotonous. Being chosen as a Signaller is by no means the only piece of luck which I have had during the period I have been serving in this War, and who knows where I would be now if it were not for the fact that I was picked out for this duty? A Signaller does no digging, guards, fatigues or dirty work; although when the Battalion is resting he has cycling duty and other work to do connected with Signalling. So much for Signalling.

Until now I had been doing Company work, "Belly flopping" (i.e. extended order drill) guards, digging, fatigues etc. but now started to master the mysteries of the Morse Code and Semaphore. A very interesting branch of a Signaller's work is map reading, and occasionally, with the aid of a map we had to find our way through certain lanes to a given point. It is by no means as simple as it sounds.

7.9.1914 and 8.9.1914

We had a Battalion Field Day on 7th September and next day the Brigade (13th County of London, The Kensingtons, 14th London Scottish, 15th Civil Service Rifles, 16th Ourselves) turned out for a Route March and the Queen's Westminsters led the Brigade.

About this time the Village Post Office found that they could not cope with the extra work which the influx of troops had occasioned and it fell to the lot of the Signallers to take over the work connected with telegrams, and tender messages to sweethearts and wives had to be left at the mercy of the Signal Service Section. I sincerely hope that all messages arrived at their destination with the wording correct, but I have my doubts.

20.9.1914

On Sunday the 20th September I had leave to go home and fetch my cycle, having been informed that it would be purchased from me for military purposes, and left in my care. I left King's Langley early in the morning with Rifleman Ford (who I am sorry to say was killed on 9th August 1915 on the Menin Road whilst carrying bombs to a captured Germ trench, during the Battle of Hooge) and took the train to Euston, and from there "taxied" to Victoria and spent the day at home. I went to St. Anselm's, Tooting Bec to church in the morning and evening. (This was to be the last I would be at home before I went to the Front, but I had no idea of this at the time.) I cycled through London to Euston with the searchlights glaring from various points. London was then fairly dark and cycling by no means too easy. On arriving back at King's Langley I cycled to the farm with Captain Challis. This Officer did not come out with us to France in November 1914, but arrived in Belgium a few days before the Battle of Hooge, returning on the day of the battle, wounded.

21.9.1914

The 2nd London Division went for a Route March on Monday the 21st September and the Artillery was also in attendance, but there is very little pleasure in a Route March of this description. It is so slow and the length of the troops in fours being so great, the unfortunate Battalions at the rear get a good meal of dust.

22.9.1914

The next day I was offered by Army Officials the sum of £5 for my bicycle[2] and I was quite willing to accept this amount. The details I will not go into, but considering the length of time I had had the cycle and the amount of travelling I had done on it, it was quite a reasonable figure (from my point of view). We did not get the money for some little time but we all felt very pleased with ourselves over the various sums which had been allowed for the cycles, and yarns began to leak out about certain gentlemen having bought bikes a week or two before for prices of around £3 and getting the officials to allow £6 or £7 for them. But somehow or

---

[2] To be left with me for use in carrying out my duties.

other, when it came to "paying out" things did not turn out as well as might have been expected and some of us were badly bitten. I had my amount knocked down to £3.15.0. but I could not grumble even then. It is a hard job to "do" the Army.

25.9.1914

A nasty business was the inoculation which we had to undergo on Friday the 25th September, but it gave us a couple of days in which to play cards and rest, so we could not grumble even at that.

6. Soldiers at Rest

1.10.1914

The next item of interest was the three days' firing at Hemel Hempstead, commencing on Thursday the 1st October. After I had fired my first shot, I thought the world had come to an end. The "kick" of the rifle gave me an awful hit on the jaw and also bruised my shoulder badly. Of course the moral is to hold one's rifle tightly.

I got a good "tip" and that was to put a sack under the coat by the shoulder, and so saved further trouble in this direction. I did rather well in my firing tests and when one gets used to a rifle it is very fascinating.

5.10.1914

We were inoculated again on Monday the 5th October and had another two days' rest, but at the end of these two days, who will ever forget what took place? Let me explain.

7.10.1914

At 12.35am on Wednesday 7th October, orders were received to prepare to embark and we hastened out of our "beds" and packed everything up. It was pitch dark and some of the men who had been inoculated some twelve hours before were feeling the effects rather badly, but even these turned out, as they were just as anxious as the others to go abroad as things were getting rather tame at home. Ammunition was served out, and every man took as much as possible, filling pockets and any available space, as we had heard that ammunition was scarce in France. We were all heavily laden, full packs and equipment. The Orderly Room packed up, and the transport was all ready under War conditions. The Canteens gave away their stock of Beer and Minerals, and other articles were disposed of wholesale. It is said that a certain Field Officer left a telegram at the Post Office to be dispatched first thing in the morning to his Wife, informing her of his departure.

We paraded on the Green, and a large number of the villagers turned out to wish us "Good-bye". We left about two hours after receiving our Orders, and proceeded to march to King's Langley, a distance of about four miles. All was excitement. An empty train was in a siding a mile or two from the station, and it was decided that this was for us.

Arriving at King's Langley station, we were full of expectation. After 10 minutes' wait, the order was given to the Signallers (who always lead the Battalion) "Right wheel", "Right wheel", which amounts to "About turn". We looked at one another and wondered what was happening, but thought that we were going to a siding. Our hopes, however, were dashed to the ground, for it was a false alarm![3] Let me pass over the language - it was too terrible. A stranger passing down the road the next morning must surely have thought that a terrific battle had taken place there lately, judging by the amount of ammunition he would have found strewn by the wayside. We heard later that the whole Brigade had been out. All were late as regards the train they were supposed to have caught, but the Westminsters were the "limit" being two hours over their time. 'Twas sad.

10.10.1914

On Saturday 10th October the Signallers were moved into a Farm by themselves and taken away from the Company. It was very comfortable, and the quarters were better than those in which we had been. The country around was very pretty and we had many a day's outing (pardon, Battalion and Brigade Field days), when we had to cook our own dinner. On the whole we enjoyed them immensely, especially the Signallers with their bicycles who somehow or other often managed to get lost, but they could usually be found in the local "pub".

26.10.1914

A very enjoyable afternoon was spent by us on Monday the 26th October when the Signallers went for a cycle ride through Flamstead and Radbourne. Some of us were so much behind schedule time that the Signalling Officer who waited on the road to check times etc., caught a chill leading to an illness which ultimately prevented him from coming abroad with us. Well, we can hardly be blamed, for it was a very hot day as far as cycling was concerned, and we got so very dry.

This incident proved to be the completion of our "training". As far as the Signalling section went, we knew very little of the Morse Code (which is used in France) but we were quite proficient in Semaphore (which is not used - except in emergencies).

27.10.1914

The next day, Tuesday the 27th October, definite orders were received that we were to prepare to leave England. This time it was the real thing. Again all was excitement. Our transport was

---

[3] ? We were intended for Antwerp.

condemned and we had to obtain new horses and carts; new rifles were served out and Khaki overcoats borrowed from the Civil Service Rifles in place of our grey (for the C.S.R. was not coming with us, and they eventually took over the billets at Watford which had been prepared for us for the winter). No leave was granted to Officers or men before going to the Front, although it is said an effort was made in this direction.

30.10.1914

We were to have left on Friday the 30th October, but arrangements between the War Office and the Regiment not being completed, we waited expectantly for instructions to move.

31.10.1914

On Saturday the 31st October we were inspected by the Brigadier. In the afternoon I was on Post Office duty when the Colonel handed in a telegram to say we were off to-morrow.

1.11.1914

We were all up early on Sunday the 1st November for we had plenty to do. Of course the village turned out to wish us "Good-bye". The Battalion went in two parts, the right-half-battalion under the Colonel, and the left-half-battalion under Major J.W. Cohen at 10.30am. The Band struck up "Auld Lang Syne" as the left-half-battalion moved off. Only the Signallers were left, and we dismissed for a short time and entered the "Tuck-shop", and at 11.00am left Leverstock Green on our bicycles for Watford, arriving there about 11.30am. The Battalion had a good reception when marching through the town. The transport and men being entrained, we started at 12.40pm leaving many sad hearts behind. We passed through Willesden, Basingstoke, Winchester, and arrived at Southampton about 4.30pm ("some" train). Tea was served out, and we then boarded the S.S. "MAIDAN".[4]

At Southampton there was nobody to see the men off - in fact the town knew nothing about us being near for we came straight from the train onto the quay. There was over us all a sense of loneliness, for as we looked over the side of the vessel, there were

---

[4] Burnt and sunk later in Marseilles Harbour.

only two or three seamen on the quay. However I managed to get one of them to send off a card giving the name of the ship on which we sailed. Everybody on board was strangely quiet - all the excitement had died down, and there was a tremendous calm. At 7.30pm, just as the steamer[5] commenced to slip away from the quay, somebody struck up "Auld Lang Syne" and to this tune the Queen's Westminster Rifles left England, to help in the protection of our shores. Unfortunately so many of them left it for the last time - never to return.

---

[5] An annual dinner called the Maidan Dinner is held yearly in November for those who embarked on the steamer in 1914. (Note made in 1949.)

> Q. W. R
>
> My Dear Ma,
> Just a line before I go.
> We have to entrain early tomorrow from Watford & still hope to get leave from port of Embarkment.
> I am very glad to have this experience & feel sure of my safety.
> I wired you so as to let you know.
> I have been on post office duty to-day, & sent heaps of telegrams.
> Am too busy to write more so with much love from
> Your devoted Son
> Leonard
>
> I am sending some clothes home, others have been issued. My address will be:- Rfm. L. A. Brookes, Queens West. Rfls. 16th County of Lon Battalion, 4th Infantry Brigade, 2nd London Division, British Expeditionary Force

7. Last Letter from England

Chapter 2

France

From 1st November 1914 until 31st December 1914

1.11.1914

On board the S.S. "MAIDAN" the Liverpool Scottish were also proceeding to France, and we rapidly intermixed, related various incidents to one another, and discussed War, at the same time wondering to where we were going.

I stayed on deck as we went out of the Solent, and had an opportunity to exercise my knowledge of Morse Code by reading the messages to our vessel as to her name and other particulars. Under the protection of a couple of destroyers we left the Isle of Wight behind after coming under the glare of the searchlights several times. It was a beautiful night and the sea calm, looking very fine with the reflection of the searchlights on the water. After a time it became chilly and I went below to be served with some "Bully Beef" (for the first time) and biscuits. Tea was also provided, but like many others, I could not touch it. It was not tea as we know it, but oil and tea leaves - by no means a pleasant combination. The "Dixie" (a big pot - not of a kind one sees in the City) was filled with cold water and a pipe from the engine room blew steam into the water in the pot, and in this way the water was boiled. Unfortunately the oil from the engines had made its acquaintance with the steam and every time tea was issued only a few men had any. Fortunately I had filled my water bottle at Southampton, but that did not last very long as one gets very thirsty through eating "Bully" and others who had not filled their bottles had a "nip" of mine.

Somebody managed to "get round" the steamer's cooks (who were black men), to make some coffee for which a charge of 6d was made. By the time I had heard of this, their supply had run out, and when three or four of us asked for some, they served us with water in which they had washed up the cups. We of course detected the fraud immediately, and loudly voiced our sentiments, but each of these gentlemen shook his noble head and could not (or did not want to) understand us. We were therefore 6d to the bad.

After this I thought I would try and get some rest, but my "sleeping apartments" were not as comfortable as, for instance, the Hotel Cecil. Perhaps it may be interesting to know what accommodation was like on board a troop ship at that time.

The "MAIDAN" was a cargo boat, and steps were provided for the purpose of getting down into the Holds which were the said "sleeping apartments". Round the Holds of this boat there was a narrow gangway some three or four feet wide. On account of the shortage of room, we had to lie side by side in this narrow passage. There was very little dust on the floor as the draught had blown it all away, so it was not as bad as it might have been. Most of us being taller than 4ft, we found it by no means comfortable. There was a pipe running lengthwise along the ground on which one had to lie crosswise, which position was somewhat unpleasant. However sleep did come to me at last, but I was up fairly early next morning as it was too painful to be in "kip" for any length of time.

2.11.1914

We sighted land as daylight was breaking and at 7.30am on Monday the 2nd November we stopped outside Havre. It was a beautiful day and very hot. For some reason or other we did not go into Port this day. The view outside Havre was very fine, and we could see the people on shore waving to us and apparently getting excited, waiting for our landing. We lounged about on Deck all day but we were not very happy as we were thirsty and although we made gallant attempts to drink the "tea", we could not master it, especially as we had not quite got our "sea legs" and had a funny feeling in our "Little Marys". In the evening the Westminster's and the Scottish combined and we had a jolly good concert on board, everybody joining in the choruses with great zest. After the concert and more loitering, I "turned in" and as I had had very little rest during the past night, I fell in a slumber quickly and did not wake until "Reveille" which was at 6.00am the next morning, when we found ourselves at the Quayside.

3.11.1914

At 7.00am we disembarked and then had a fairly long wait until the transport was unloaded, and the inhabitants of the town gave us much needed "Café au Lait" and hot rolls, to which we did justice. We marched through the town to the rest camp at the top of the hill behind the town, and on our way up we were heartily cheered, and all manner of gifts were bestowed upon us. A woman with a big basket of flowers either gave them all away or else pinned them on the men as they marched along. This shows the spirit of the people at that time. It seems that we were practically the first British troops landed at Havre, the previous base being St. Nazaire. After a meal we were feeling much better, but permission could not be obtained to go into the town in case orders were received to move, but somehow or other I managed to wander out and was collared by a Lady and her daughter, and I had a long chat with them in French. I then had a knowledge of French, the style taught in schools, and the Lady being rather excitable spoke hurriedly for about half an hour, and I must honestly say that I hardly understood a word about what she was telling me. However I tried to look intelligent and now and then, when a pause presented an opportunity (which was by no means too often) I said "Oui c'est vrai" or "Non Madam". The daughter rather entered into the fun of the business, being able to see that I could not gather much of what was being said, and when she did get a chance of speaking with me, she spoke slowly and distinctly, and I was able to understand her quite well. I got on nicely with the daughter.

4.11.1914

We were to have stayed three days at the Rest Camp, but as the voyage had been fairly smooth and we were wanted up the Line, we left Havre the next day, Wednesday the 4th November at 3.30pm, and again marched through the town to the Railway Station. On our way we passed the Kensingtons (13th London Regiment) who had just arrived from England. We waited on the station in the rain for about five hours, and in the meantime saw some Germ prisoners

A SIGNALLER'S WAR

who were brought in, and we were struck by the youthfulness of a number of them. I am not going to say that it was typical of the Germ Army at that time, but the fact remains that there were some who were little more than boys.

At 9.15pm our "train" left Havre, and perhaps it may be as well to define the word "train" in this instance. It consisted of a number of carriages marked in white paint "pour 20 chevaux", but thank goodness they had been well washed out, and about 40 "Hommes" managed to get into each. Again the sleeping accommodation left much to be desired, and the carriages being devoid of springs, we got the full benefit of the jerking of the train.

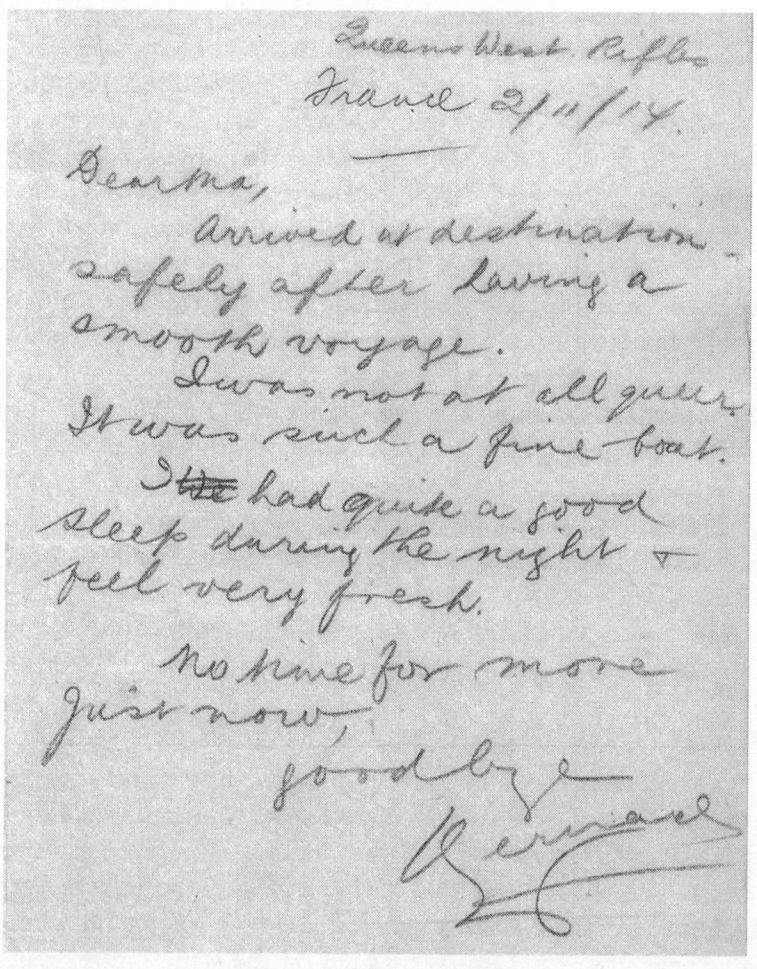

8. First Letter from France

5.11.1914

We passed through Rouen and at 7.30am the next day the 5th November, the train stopped for half-an-hour near a small brook by the side of the line, so we had a good wash and felt much better for it. We had a meal of biscuits and "Bully" on the way which we washed down with Café au Lait, French Biere, or Wine which we managed to get at some of the stations at which the train stopped for water etc. Every time the train stopped there was a rush out of the carriage to a shop nearby and many of the villagers went short of bread, for we took no refusal. Many narrow escapes of missing the train could be reported, but as the train by no means exceeded the speed limit, one could, by a sharp walk, overtake it after the style of the S.E.&C.R.

After passing through Abancourt, Anmale, Martinville, Oisemond, Allery and Longpré, we arrived at Abbeville about midday where the train stopped for an hour, and it allowed us time to drop into a "magasin" near the station and to get some bread, cheese and chocolate in lieu of the usual "Bully" on which we had been feeding practically all the time since leaving England, except whilst we were at the Rest Camp.

After leaving Abbeville we "carried on" and passed Etaples and Boulogne, arriving at Calais about 9.00pm. Here there was a deal of confusion. Having been in the train for a matter of 24 hours, we got out of our carriages onto the line where hot Bovril was awaiting us which the transport officer at Calais had provided. We all thought we had reached our destination, and as at that time the Germs were not so very far from Calais we anticipated going into a scrap within a short space of time. It must be remembered that we knew practically nothing of the real conditions. We had not been stationary for more than three minutes, and were in the middle of our Bovril when the train commenced to move out of the station in the direction in which we had come, and we did not know whether we were backing into another siding or whether we ought to get into the train again. However a few boarded (I amongst them) but a considerable number stayed behind. Strangely enough we travelled at a very high rate of speed, and then came to the conclusion, which proved to be correct, that the engine had shifted to the other end of the train and we were continuing our journey, not having reached our destination. A number of rumours then started – (the Army is full of them) – the chief being that whilst we were in the train the Germs had advanced and were near Calais, and we were being sent back in case the town fell completely into their hands, and we were not yet considered to be trained enough to take our place in the firing line.

I was fairly "fed up" with travelling, and during this discussion fell into slumber, as also did most of the others. We woke after a couple of hours to find ourselves in a siding, but where was a mystery. Eventually the word was passed down that we were at St. Omer, the Headquarters of Sir John French and his staff. We were ordered to detrain, and enquiries were being made as to the number of men missing, when another train came in with the absentees, the Transport Officer at Calais having done the necessary with great promptitude. The carriages being emptied of our stores, bicycles etc., we "fell in" and left the station at 12.30am next morning (or in other words in the middle of the night).

Incidentally I led the Battalion with my cycle. We proceeded to the Infantry Barracks at the top of the hill, and after an issue of rum (for the first time) we "turned in". These Barracks were by no means too clean or comfortable.

6.11.1914

With regard to Rum, perhaps a few words would not be out of place. The people who have voiced the opinion (from an armchair by the fireside at home, possibly) that the issue of Rum to men at the Front should be discontinued, surely do not know how necessary it is, and how often it is the means of saving life. When one has not a comfortable fire by which to sit, brandy balls will not suffice to keep out the cold, and Rum in its way takes the place of a fire in that it so thoroughly warms the body. Many a time when in the Trenches during the winter standing knee-deep in mud and water, the only thing which keeps a man alive is Rum. I have never come across an Infantryman who has been in the Trenches during the winter who is against the issue of Rum, but if there is such a one he need not have it. Personally I am not fond of it as a drink, but without it on a cold night conditions would be far worse than they are at present. It is quite true that before an attack a bigger issue of Rum is allowed each man "to get his back up", but if the men don't object, why worry? Let these fireside gentlemen try a "wee" drop, and perhaps they may begin to like it.

After sleeping until about 7.00am I went round to see the Cathedral in the town. There is a beautiful side chapel designated "The Altar of Miracles" and around the walls are tablets which have been erected by people in thanksgiving for some favour received. It is indeed a beautiful Cathedral, and being the first Continental Cathedral I had entered, I was struck by the difference in design and general appearance from our Cathedrals in England, many of which I have visited. When I entered, a service was in progress, and one might have imagined that a Requiem was being celebrated for there were so many people in black clothing and it was so noticeable. There was far more black here than I have seen since I returned to England. St. Omer evidently had already paid the price. Men too were more scarce in the Churches and Towns in France than in England.

On return to Barracks I saw Field Marshal Sir John French who had been talking with some of our men.

During the afternoon a party of the "Royal Irish Regiment" attempted (and fairly well succeeded) in "putting the wind up" our fellows. They had just returned from the firing line to reorganise, having been rather severely "cut up". Many yarns were spun, the details of which I now know to have been doubtful. Since then however, I have told newcomers even worse (if possible), for somehow or other, when one soldier speaks to another about the War and personal experiences connected with it, each tries to outdo the other, and "Freshers" are always so eager to hear tales of the Front, that the biggest liar always gets the largest audience. I have often collected a good crowd.

The various statements of the Royal Irish led us to believe that the War would be over within a month or two, or at any rate before Christmas, but it must be remembered that they had returned just about the time when the Germs had been driven back a good distance, and these men thought that they were still "on the run". We were therefore rather anxious to "get into it", for as we said to each other: "It will be awful returning home without having done anything". Our fears, however, were without the slightest foundation.

We learnt that the Germ Infantry had been at St. Omer, and were in possession of the Railway Station for a period of seven hours until they met the British troops, when they hastily retreated, being only a small advance guard.

7.11.1914

The next day, Saturday the 7th November, the Battalion marched, (Signallers cycled), some five miles out of St. Omer in the direction of the firing line, (we were many miles from the trenches), and on a hill which we mounted, we could hear the roar of the guns very distinctly. They seemed plentiful, and I think we somewhat lost our anxiety about getting to the Front. The Battalion dug trenches; The Signallers waited for any work which might turn up, and looked after their bicycles. Aeroplanes were travelling overhead, flying very low, with red, white and blue rings plainly showing. We returned at six o'clock.

8.11.1914

Early next morning, Sunday the 8th November, we paraded and marched to a portion of flat country, where the Battalion did some "belly flopping" for practice, which lasted all day. The Signallers, as usual, did "na poo". To give the stretcher-bearers a chance of exercising their skill, it was arranged that, now and then, a man should not rise from the ground, and be treated as a casualty. He would tell the stretcher-bearers that he was shot through the leg, for instance, and they would proceed to bandage his wound. He would then be allowed to stay behind, and do as much work as the Signallers. As the day wore on, so many of the men failed to rise, that the S.B. could not cope with the work, and when the Commanding Officer saw the number who were being "treated", he made each man re-join his Company, and put them through some stiff training. After this incident it was left to the Company Officers to detail men as casualties.

The wind was blowing from the direction of the Firing Line, and the sound of the guns was much plainer. About 3.30pm a violent bombardment started, which continued until after six o'clock.

9.11.1914

Whilst London was watching the Lord Mayor's Show on the 9th November 1914, we were out again for the day doing practically the same as previously. Already the men were feeling the effects of the past few days and a number were ill. Amongst this number was Croxford who joined with me, and he was sent to Hospital.[6]

10.11.1914

At 8.00am next morning, Tuesday the 10th November, I left St. Omer with three other Signalling Cyclists and Major Cohen, on horseback, en route for Hazebrouck, to arrange billets for the Battalion which was coming on later in the day. The roads were awful, all the cobbles being slippery there having been a fall of rain during the night. It was quite hard enough cycling, and it must have been much worse marching. On reaching Epeques we dismounted in reverence to a funeral which was passing at the time. A French funeral is very different from one which might be seen in English streets. A procession is formed at the house, and taking the lead is a man in Cassock and Surplice bearing a large Crucifix. Then a number of boys similarly dressed, the Priest praying, the coffin and a large number of people of the place who care to take part, and they all walk to the Church and then to the Cemetery. It is very impressive.

At 11.00am we arrived at Hazebrouck having travelled some 15 miles, and as we entered the town and saw a sight which brought tears to my eyes, and I will never forget it. From the direction of the Firing Line came streams of men, women and children, carrying all they could with them, having had to leave their homes. Very stained and weather-beaten, for they had been walking for a long time, having had to rush away from their houses, risking their lives from shell and rifle fire. They carried large bundles filled with articles (some had a blanket-full on their back) and they were crying enough to break their hearts. We got into communication with them, and they informed us that the Germs, who had taken all food and everything of value from them, were again advancing. Many of them had been in Germs' hands for some time, and they told us many woeful tales. It is as sad a sight as one could possibly see.

The Germs had not so very long ago been at Hazebrouck and food was therefore very scarce. What had been left was sold in the shops at greatly inflated prices.

The Battalion arrived later and the Signallers showed them their billets.

---

[6] ? Scarlet Fever.

11.11.1914

At 9.30am next morning, Wednesday 11th November, we departed from Hazebrouck, leaving one section of "E" Company behind on account of an outbreak of fever. We passed through the village of Borre, and arrived at Bailleul at midday. We were to have gone on further, but there was a strong wind and a drizzle, and the cobbled roads were proving too much for the feet (I cycled) that the Colonel decided to put up here. The march had been very difficult inasmuch that the ranks had to be broken several times to allow A.S.C. Motor Transports to pass, the road being very narrow. This helped to make the marching harder.

The transport of the Battalion was missing, and a Signaller named Chamberlain and I were "told off" to find them. We went a few miles back but could not discover any trace, and after staggering some villagers by asking them in French if they had seen anything of them, we found an Estaminet, where we drank of the "loving cup" and dried our clothes. When we returned to Bailleul the transport had arrived and the men were in their Billets, in a Convent.

The Germs had left many indications of their arrival by the damage which the Town had sustained, broken telegraph wires, smashed doors etc., but there were no shell holes, as only a body of Infantry had passed through, the Artillery not having time to get up before they were driven from St. Omer, right back at the point of the bayonet.

It rained towards evening, and the Town was very miserable, so many people having left their Homes, and other than Soldiers, there was hardly anybody else in the streets. There was an Estaminet or two open, and we called in for a beverage, and were told that although the Germs had only been a week in the place, they had practically consumed every available drop of alcohol, the men paying nothing, and the Officers giving IOUs! The proprietor of one establishment however, had managed to hide a quantity, which he said he had kept for the time when the "Soldats Anglais" would drive the Germs out and all he had he was willing to give away to us for "rein de tout". We did not take advantage of this offer, as he had lost so much money and other valuables, and we paid him a price.

12.11.1914

At 9.30am the next day, Thursday the 12th November we again got on the move, and enroute passed through Steenwerck with its fine Church and spire; and Croix-du-Bac where the Church had been fired by the Germs and razed to the ground. Houses on the road were similarly treated, many of them being ruined beyond repair.

Erquinghem proved to be our destination, which we reached after being spotted by a Germ aeroplane (for we were now only two or three miles from the nearest point of the Firing Line) and for the first time became acquainted with shrapnel, but all the shells fell short and no damage was done. The distance we had travelled was about 12 miles and along the road we had passed many more refugees, but they were now a common sight and little notice was taken of them. It is so easy to forget trouble when one's self is not concerned, and we had other matters to think about.

As soon as we arrived we were informed that as Lord Roberts was nearby, he was going to inspect us. We therefore had a quick dinner and prepared to make ourselves clean and smart and try to look like soldiers. We lined the streets, causing much excitement amongst the folk who were still there, probably because they were too old to move or had no money and nothing to lose, even if the Germs did get through again, and at two o'clock Lord Roberts came past, addressing a few words now and then to some of us. This was his last function, for on this day he contracted a chill, which led to his death two days later, not far behind the firing line. He died doing his duty, as such a Soldier would wish, and may he rest in peace.[7]

We were billeted in one part of a school, and another portion was crowded with refugees, men, women and children altogether, who were always asking us for food we could not eat, or which was left over. They were sent further back the next day and we took over their quarters after they had had a good clean out.

We were allowed in the village, but had to take a rifle with ammunition, on account of spies, shots having been fired at troops before, from houses in the neighbourhood. It rained later in the afternoon, but towards the close of the day I went out to the end of the village street and watched shrapnel bursting in the air near

---

[7] ? Died in Armentières or St Omer.

Armentières (on the left of Erquinghem, about two miles from the firing line). Several buildings were on fire caused by incendiary shells which the Germs had sent into the town. The bursting of shells at night when the clouds are low is a very fine sight, and would be full of interest if the results were not so tragic.

Our sleep was badly disturbed during the night by a heavy cannonade, which started in the early hours of the morning and continued until late in the afternoon.

13.11.1914

The Battalion went out next morning and dug some trenches in front of the railway station. These were necessary, as the British only had one line of trenches, and none to fall back on should the Germs again advance. As soon as the rainy season set in seriously, the second and third lines of trenches were swamped and during the greater part of the winter we only had the one line, but it is practically impossible for an attack to be successful when there is so much mud, as the men get stuck and make a fine target for a rifle or machine gun. Whilst this digging was in progress the rain commenced and a strong gale sprung up, but the Signallers were snug and comfortable in a barn out of the way, waiting in case they were wanted.

In the evening a visit was paid to the local Estaminet where Mademoiselle Alice [8] made us nice and comfortable.

14.11.1914

The guns started again early the next morning, but we were getting used to them by this time, and it affected our sleep only slightly. The weather being finer, aeroplanes were busy, and for a large portion of the day, we were staring open-mouthed at the sky, watching small puffs of smoke as shells burst around the aeroplanes.

15.11.1914

Sunday, the 15th November saw me at my duties at the small village Church, where the youngsters had an opportunity of shouting enough to seriously injure the lungs of an ordinary

---

[8] Wrong, I think Alice was at Houplines.

individual. At all the services I attended in France, the congregation, and especially the boys, seemed to make a point of shouting as loudly as they could, instead of singing. Congregational singing is the order of the day, but it seemed to me that every person tried to out-do his or her neighbour in the matter of shouting.

A sermon was preached to the accompaniment of the boom of the guns a couple of miles away, and on the whole it helped to make the service very impressive. Every now and again one could feel the Church actually shake when a big gun was fired.

After the British troops had driven the Germs back through Erquinghem, a few Germs had remained in the Belfry of the Church with a supply of food, machine guns and rifles, and when a body of soldiers passed, shots were fired. At first it was not discovered from whence the firing proceeded. The Germ artillery was also very smart in catching bodies of men who might be marching up the road. The hands of the clock having been seen to move rapidly, a search was made and these men were found in the tower, having used the hands for Signalling in Semaphore, which accounted for the fact that the main body of the Germs knew so well when troops were moving, and through an aperture in the clock they had fired when men were passing. I will not say what became of these men, but when I was there the clock face was shifted to one side, so preventing further tampering. From six o'clock, for a period of about 30 minutes a deafening cannonade was started by the guns, and we watched the flashes as they were fired, standing in awed groups, wondering when it would end.

16.11.1914

Monday, the 16th November, was rather quieter, although Armentières was heavily shelled intermittently. I was on cycling duty all day in the rain. Some cottages were set on fire by the Germs, the shells killing all the inhabitants. Part of the Battalion moved up, preparatory to entering the trenches for the first time, but the Company with which I was, stayed behind.

17.11.1914

The remainder anticipated going to the trenches today and at 7.00am I went to Church to prepare myself for the worst. During the morning however, orders came out, that all the Battalion left behind, except my Company (for although I was a Signaller I had been with the Company for the sake of convenience since leaving England) were to go to the trenches that night and that we were to be isolated on account of another man having a touch of fever. We could have "bitten our heads off" with disappointment when seeing the men leave for Griespot, and the trenches at Bois Grenier, a distance of four or five miles. However, we had to be content during the day with watching aeroplanes being shelled. Our work was physical drill.

9. Armentières

18.11.1914

Orders were received the next day that no man was allowed out so as not to spread any illness, and that we would have a medical inspection every day. I had to go out being on cycling duty, so I did not have such a bad time. During the afternoon a spy was brought in to us. He had been caught in the act of shooting our men not far behind our own lines. He did not live long to tell the tale.

19.11.1914

The next day we went for a route march in the snow to keep us in a fit state of health. Our first casualty was also reported this day, and strange to say the man who was killed (through the falling in of his "dug-out") bore the same name as mine but Brooks. His brother who was in the same shelter had his leg broken. The similarity of names caused a fright at home, but upon inquiries being made at our Headquarters in London happiness was again restored to the family bosom, but unfortunately it informed them vividly that I had got into the danger zone and I had so far managed not to let them know that I was near the firing line. In the evening we had a good concert round the fire.

> **THE QUEEN'S WESTMINSTERS.**
>
> The following casualties in the Queen's Westminster Battalion at the front have been officially notified:—
>
> Killed in Action.—R. Brooks and R. D. Tucker.
> Died of Wounds.—J. Cunnington.
> Wounded, notified on December 10.—Rifleman Mayhew, gunshot wound in head; Corporal J. G. Weller, in left hand; Rifleman H. Morfey, in right shoulder. Notified on December 15.—Rifleman J. M. Constable, wounded in both hands; W. J. Wright, hand and left lung; J. G. Walkington, lip; C. W. Phipp, shoulder; F. N. Tyler, leg; P. G. Diggens, arm; and J. D. Feldwicke, back.

10. Queen's Westminster Battalion Casualties

20.11.1914

It was very cold today and snowing fast, but we turned out and practised range-finding. In the evening there was a gorgeous sunset. I might mention that never have I seen finer sunsets than in this part of France. In the trenches, one having plenty of time in which to look round, perhaps the sunsets are more noticeable than in England, but I think that the country being so flat has an effect of making it possible to see such fine sunsets.

We continued doing the work mentioned above with very little variation until the end of the month, by which time we were absolutely "fed". On one of our route marches we noticed a dog working a mill, and another pulling a small cart, and other incidents showed us how, in France, dogs are used for purposes such as we would not think of in England.

Our transport was a mile or two back, and every day some men had to be on guard there. A farm was a short distance away but too far for sleeping, so we had to make our beds in a haystack, and although it certainly was my first experience of so sleeping, I would recommend it in the case of a better substitute not being available.

Of course the rats were rather unpleasant but one can get used to them, as we had to in the trenches. At any rate I was by no means pleased when called at 2.00am to turn out for a couple of hours' guard.

28.11.1914

On Saturday the 28th November the men whom we had left at Hazebrouck turned up, having been declared free from any infection. They had taken the train to Steenwerck and so avoided the very unpleasant march. They rested for a short time at Erquinghem and then went on to the trenches, so once more we cursed our luck.

We cannot honestly say that we were well trained soldiers, and as a matter of fact we were rather surprised that the Battalion had so quickly been sent up to the front, instead of (as anticipated) on lines of communication. As an illustration; one man who was loading his rifle preparatory to leaving for the trenches was holding it with the barrel pointing upwards instead of to the ground. He[9] pressed the trigger and a bullet flew out which narrowly missed the head of the Colour Sergeant,[10] who I am afraid had rather a fright at having his baptism of fire before it was expected.

During the night the Germans made themselves very objectionable and started shelling near to us. We did not turn out, but the "Buffs" (East Kent Regiment) were shelled out of their billets where they were having a well-earned rest from the trenches.

30.11.1914

I had to cycle next day into Armentières on duty, so got an opportunity of looking over the town and Cathedral. There were very few people left in Armentières at that time, (but they returned before I left France for Belgium in May 1915, as they no doubt felt sure that the Germs would not get the British out of their trenches) and considerable damage was done to the Cathedral and other churches, (there are six or seven large churches here) which at the time I thought was very serious. Since having seen Ypres, however, it strikes me that Armentières has so far been very fortunate inasmuch that the firing line in parts is not more than a mile or so

---

[9] Turnbull.
[10] Since killed in action.

away from the town, whereas at Ypres I should estimate the nearest point of the Germ line would be three miles.

Our men who had gone to the trenches on 16th November, came out early this morning and I met some of them in Armentières and they gave me their opinion of the War in language which I will not repeat here, but I did not feel so sorry that I had not yet gone to them. They had had about half-a-dozen casualties and had been in the trenches for 14 days, which, considering the weather was rather stiff for the first entry, but at any rate their opinions had greatly changed and none wanted another spell in the trenches for some time.

2.12.1914

His Majesty the King was near Erquinghem on 2nd December, and he inspected some of the Westminsters just after they had come out of the trenches in mud arrayed, so he saw to a certain extent what Londoners were doing for him and our country.

7.12.1914

We were to be isolated until 14 days after the last outbreak and were informed on Monday 7th December that, provided no other man was ill, we would be going into the trenches on 9th December.

To have some stiff exercise before going into the trenches, we went for a route march today and it commenced to rain, so that we got a good soaking. During the afternoon it cleared up, and as I was feeling rather miserable, being wet and cold, I found an excuse for a cycle ride into Armentières, and had a good look round another part of the town which before I had not seen.

On returning I heard that there was an opportunity of a warm bath (which I had not been able to have since I left England) and three of us got out of billets to find a brewery which had been converted into a bathing establishment, and we were informed that a few coppers to the R.A.M.C. man in charge would permit of us having a bath, although actually only parties were allowed, when about ten or a dozen men could get into a tub together.

We walked four or five miles and dusk came on, but we could not discover the bathhouse. We had to give it up in the end, and "turned about" to be met with rain, beating heavily against our faces, and a strong gale which made it impossible to hear one another's voice. Added to this it was pitch dark. Such a night I have never before experienced. We did not know our way, and it took us about four hours to get back to our billet, and when we did we had to sleep through the night in our wet clothes.

11. Erquinghem Station

8.12.1914

We were told definitely on Tuesday the 8th December that we were to go nearer the firing line that day, and before long, into the trenches, and our hearts beat high. At 3.30pm we started out and marched to L'Armée, where we met the rest of the Battalion.

L'Armée, a village, was too small and unsafe to stay in, so we found a farm nearby for the night, and to this we proceeded. After tea the Company (without the Signallers) had to go to the trenches for four hours' digging under fire, and I am sorry to say that two men did not return, they having already ended their experience of War rather quickly and tragically.

We "turned in" in a small loft capable of holding about 20 men, and at 2.00am about 40 others came back from digging and had to sleep with us. However, we squeezed in and although it was a bitterly cold night and raining hard, I do not think I have ever been so hot before in my life, so it had the advantage of keeping out the cold. Rum had been served out, and the heat of the place made some of the men rather groggy, and when they had to get up during the night for Guard, or other reasons, much jumping on legs was occasioned, which of course roused everybody in the Barn and at times the atmosphere was quite thick through the fluency of the language.

9.12.1914

We got up next morning rather later than was usual, and this foretold that we were for the trenches that night. The whole Battalion went to the Baths, and to use a soldier's expression, "That did it". Let me explain, and at the same time apologise for mentioning a matter which is very unpleasant but nevertheless quite true, and an important feature in the discomforts which one has to undergo at the front.

After the bath, the dirty clothes are given in and "clean" washing issued out to all the men. For a short time all is well. On the march back one gets rather warm and a careful observer will notice a large amount of wriggling and scratching going on, and then the men realise that they are "chatty" or "crummy." Of course at first it is exceedingly unpleasant and repulsive, but like so many other things, one has to get used to this state, and once started it is almost impossible to get rid of these objectionable livestock. For eight months I was in this state.

After dinner there was plenty for the Signallers to do, as we were off to the trenches that night and by the time I had finished my cycling duty, the Battalion had left. I was rather in a "stew" and made inquiries as to the direction taken and managed, on my cycle, to catch up with my Company about half a mile behind the firing line. I was told that I had to go back, find the Dressing Station (First Aid Post) leave my cycle there and come to the trenches with the stretcher bearers, who knew the way.

On arriving at the Dressing Station I was instructed where to put my cycle, but the stretcher-bearers had gone, and I was stranded. Over the wire I was informed that on account of the fever scare I was not to go to a Signalling Station, but to remain with the Company, and that as there was a shortage of men, I was to come down that night. My directions were as follows:

"Straight up the road until a barrier of two carts is reached, and 50 yards past the barrier there is an opening in the hedge which leads on to a field. By going at right angles with the road, a farm would be sited, and then inquire again."

It was now about 8.00pm, and I started with full pack, 250 rounds of ammunition (which weigh very heavily), rifle, blanket (wrapped in my waterproof sheet) slung over my back, and overcoat on, for it was raining; feeling well loaded. There was a slight fog, and it was pitch black, except that now and again a flare would shine dimly through the mist, dying out, and making the darkness still more intense.

I proceeded along the road past Chappelle d'Armentières, and bumped against the barrier, thereby knowing that I was on the right track. The bullets were flying around, and being alone, I did not feel quite comfortable. I was very warm, so I halted behind the carts for a rest, during which time, the Durham Light Infantry, who we relieved came from the trenches, and one or two stragglers told me that one of our officers[11] had been shot going up, and a few seconds later he came along on a stretcher. This did not make me feel any more comfortable, and I began to wish that I had somebody with me.

I pulled myself together, and got on until I came across the opening of which I had been told, and entered. My first few steps took me knee deep in mud, and being such hard work over the ploughed fields in this condition, I was perspiring freely. I dared not get off the beaten track in case I should miss the farm. After a distance which seemed terribly long and hard (for every time I heard a rifle shot I "ducked", which made my pack and blanket shift into a most uncomfortable position) at last, through the fog, I spotted the farm. I took shelter behind a wall which had a good share of shell holes, and then I heard some very queer noises proceeding from the other side. After a few seconds it stopped - was it somebody in pain who had been hit? - and again it started, so I went round to investigate and, joy of joys, I found a soldier filling a rum jar with water from a very old and rusty pump.

I enquired the way to the part of the trenches which were being occupied by the Queen's Westminsters. His reply to the effect that he had never heard of them, rather upset my dignity. I told him that we were relieving the Durham Light Infantry, and he directed me to follow by the side of a communication trench, which was full of water and did not permit of one using it, for five hundred yards; and I would then arrive at my destination.

---

[11] ? Townsend Green who was our first officer wounded.

I found that the communication trench (or rather ditch) which I had been following, broke off in two directions about 50 yards from the farm, but as he said that we were on the right, I followed along what I afterwards discovered was an old front line trench. However, I did not know this at the time, and I continued on my way.

I must have gone nearly a mile before I came to the conclusion that something was wrong, and I became desperate. The "whiz" of the bullets told me that I was going parallel with the trenches, so I struck off at right angles across a field, hoping to meet somebody. I had not gone more than 50 yards when I saw a light. My heart beat rapidly - where was I? Were these the British or Germ trenches? I laid down flat in the mud and listened, and heard such language which perhaps at ordinary times might make me blush, but now it was like the sound of sweet music. I went nearer making such remarks as "I say, old chap" very quietly for I did not know where the Germs were, and I was "some windy". No notice was taken of my remark, for I was outside the trench and no doubt I spoke too softly to be heard. I went nearer and put one foot inside the trench when a gruff voice shouted "who the - - - hell are you?" I explained that I was in the Queen's Westminster Rifles, but that did not seem to satisfy him as he had never heard the name of our regiment. After explanations and a chat with an Officer who gave me a tot of rum, I was informed that I would have to go about a mile to the left, and that, as the trenches in parts were full of water, I had better get out again and walk along the top. Once inside, I did not quite like the idea of being on top again, but as there were some men about, it was not so bad. The Germs, I was told, were some four or five hundred yards in front.

I got out and crossed some fields, being challenged several times, and asking if I was going in the correct direction, when at last I came across my Battalion about 10.30pm saying a sincere prayer, and heaving a sigh of relief. I had the only "dug-out" left, and it was very badly built, the bottom being under the level of the trenches, the result was about three inches of mud and water. At that time I did not know the way to construct a good "dug-out" (or "buggy-hutch" as it is called) otherwise I might have built another, although the ground being so wet and there being no wood available then, as there is now for such purposes, I might not have made a great success of it. However I put my waterproof sheet on the ground, and was thankful to get my pack, blankets, and equipment off my back.

No sooner had I done this when I was told that I was on ration fatigue and had to go out of the trenches twice again to the farm, and bring in a sack of coke and a tin of tea. By this time I was wet through to the skin, and it was near midnight, and I thought that I would be able to get some rest, but I was deceived for, on my return, I had two hours' guard to do. At 1.30am I was detailed to form one of a party to relieve others who were trench digging out in front. A new trench was being made as our present one in places had 6ft of water in it. So, as soon as I had finished my guard, about 2.00am, I went about 50 yards in front of our line in the rain and mist to help in the making of a new trench.

"C'EST LA GUERRE, MAIS CE N'EST PAS MAGNIFIQUE"
The interior of a signal "office" somewhere in France.—Time: 2 a.m.
BY TROOPER J. G. COWELL, WARWICKSHIRE YEOMANRY

12. Cartoon

I had done some digging in England, which permitted an occasional rest, but when digging under fire it is a different tale altogether. In the previous party two men had been hit, and we had to dig deep enough to get into the hole under cover, and then make up the line. We dug with feverish haste, and were getting on well, when the man[12] next to me, (who happened to be the fellow I had slept next to in the Erquinghem schools) was shot, and he died before the stretcher bearers had got him to the Dressing Station.[13] This naturally made me dig harder than ever until I thought that my arms would drop out of their sockets. We had to get to a certain depth before dawn for the trench had to be improved, and when the Germs spotted in the morning that we had been working, they would make a point of firing heavily all the next night in the hope of catching the working party. We therefore kept going until about 4.30am when we went back to our old trenches and turned in for a rest. I had got nicely off to sleep (in spite of the wet) when at 5.15am we were roused for the "stand to" which takes place before dawn and sunset each day, as this is the time it is most likely for an attack to be delivered.

10.12.1914

We "stood down" after a couple of hours, and then had to clean our rifles and swords, which in every case were covered with mud and rust. This is by no means an easy job when one's supply of rifle rag is scarce and muddy. It was now 8.00am and we started on "Bully", biscuits, jam, and water (we had no wood to light a fire to boil Tea) which we consumed together with a fair supply of mud. After breakfast and inspection of rifles the trench had to be cleared and the water bailed out as much as possible, and portions which had fallen in during the night had to be banked up. I then went on Guard for an hour, which brought us near dinner-time. By way of a change the menu was altered to biscuits, "Bully", water, and Jam. After dinner I had a couple of hours' rest until the evening "stand to" and then we had tea of jam, biscuits, mud, water, with a drop of rum, (another change of diet). During the night I did two hours' digging, and four hours' guard, for which considering the "night" started at 4.00pm gave me more rest.

It rained during the afternoon and I was beginning to feel the cold, which was very severe.[14] As a matter of fact these trenches

---

[12] ? Weston.
[13] We had no tin hats in those days.
[14] Trenches themselves were 1ft-2ft deep in water. We had to climb on to the fire step to

were the worst I have ever been in whether winter or summer, so perhaps there is some excuse when I say that by this time I was very miserable and as anxious to get out of the trenches, as I had been to get in, although my occupation had been so short a time.

14.12.1914

This is the general outline of what took place every day, with a few casualties, until 14th December, when at 1.15am the Germs started a heavy cannonade of shell and rifle fire on our right which necessitated our being on guard all through the night. The Germ artillery set fire to two farms in our immediate rear which gave such a glare that it prevented the men from bringing up the rations for the next day as they had to come overland, the communication trenches being flooded. As a matter of fact during the winter the communication trenches are very seldom used as travelling is so difficult and even in the summer men prefer to walk across fields to the front line rather than use the communication trenches, as there are so many twists and turns in a communication trench that very often the distance is doubled. The turns (or "traverses") are to prevent a shell, should it burst in the trench, from going right along the line. These traverses being about 10 feet one from the other, the damage of the shell would be confined to this space.

During the night I had rather a narrow shave. My rifle, with bayonet fixed, was pointing through my loophole and when I moved a couple of yards away to get at the mug of rum which I was sharing with the man next to me, a bullet hit my rifle smashing both my sword and barrel. If I had been standing behind, I would not like to say where the destination of the bullet would have been.

15.12.1914

The next day we had more rain and the trenches were flooded. During the afternoon I took off my greatcoat to scrape the mud away which was adhering and making the coat weigh very heavily. I must have lifted it slightly in the air for I had just put it on top of my dug-out, when - "ping" - it was hit by a bullet which embedded itself a foot of two in the mud. I dug that bullet out to keep as a souvenir, but when I returned to England it was left in my pack, and I have not recovered it.

---

move about.

A large number of men by this time were suffering from such complaints as Rheumatism, Frost Bite, Trench Feet, and suchlike, which caused them to be removed from the trenches and many got back to England. The cold had been very intense, and we had been standing in water, at times up to our hips, whilst the rest of our clothing was soaked through. We had slept in this state, and had no wash since entering the trenches, so it can hardly be wondered at that there was illness about. Now that I look back and think of my first experience of the trenches, which was certainly the worst, I really cannot understand how I am alive to tell the tale. Apart from the risk of being shot, being in wet clothes for so long a period is serious, and when at home on a rainy night, one takes elaborate precautions against cold if the feet get slightly wet, whereas out there no notice whatever can be taken of the elements. It is marvellous that we did not all have Rheumatic Fever at the very least, and although I did have a touch of Rheumatism, it was not serious enough for me to have to leave the trench but only added a little more misery to my already unhappy condition.

17.12.1914

I am by no means mentioning all our casualties for then this would be too painful reading, but worthy of mention was a stretcher bearer who was killed on Thursday 17th December by a shell, whilst attending to a wounded comrade.

18.12.1914

We were relieved from the trenches in the evening of the Friday the 18th December by the Royal Fusiliers, after a period of nine days which was quite enough for me. At this time we were attached to the 7th Division until our Brigade could make arrangements for us to join them and we had no sooner got into billets (empty houses full of shell holes) in Chappelle d'Armentières, when a great deal of activity sprung up opposite the part of the line held by the Seventh Division and we had to "stand to", which meant another night without taking off our boots and clothes and sleeping in equipment, as if in the trenches.

19.12.1914

The next morning we took off our wet clothes, had a good wash, scraped the mud off our jackets, overcoats, puttees, cleaned rifles, opened parcels from home and had a good feed. (Letters and small parcels are delivered in the trenches when possible.) When in the middle of these undertakings the Germs shelled the billets occupied by "A" Company and a shell fell in the middle of a room in which a rifle inspection was being held, killing three or four and wounding others. It is not only in the trenches where there is danger but anywhere near the firing line, and one is never sure of his life from the time first going to the trenches, until one leaves for a real rest, which in our case was not granted whilst I was with the Battalion in Flanders, a period of nearly 10 months.

20.12.1914

Our clothes were useless even after the mud had been scraped off, therefore next day, Sunday the 20th December, we were issued with new clothing and boots and felt more comfortable than we had for a long time. At 4.00pm we were called up to act as reserves to the firing line, and marched to a barn 50 yards behind the front trenches and slept there during the night, leaving before dusk next morning.

22.12.1914

Tuesday the 22nd December saw me back with the Signal Service Section and I was very thankful, for I did not want another turn in the trenches such as I had gone through and I felt sorry for the other men who were not as fortunate as I. It was not very long before I started on my Signalling duties, in the afternoon being detailed to go with one Company who were to be reserves in the Farm where I had been with my Company two days previously and I took my cycle in case there was an attack, no Telegraph wires being laid on at this point of the line. My duty if an attack were made, would be to fetch reinforcements. I started out about an hour after the Company, another cyclist having gone with them. I passed the railway line at Chappelle d'Armentières and turned to the left down a road running parallel with the lines. About half way along the length of this road one came under range of rifle fire, but having now got used to bullets being nearby, and being on my cycle,

I did not have uncomfortable feelings such as I had before. As a matter of fact I was feeling very happy and contented as I had rejoined the Signal Section, and I quite enjoyed the sensation of cycling under fire for the first time. It is full of excitement as is apparent from the following. I turned to the right at the end of the road, and the farm for which I was making was a matter of 100 yards along (I knew my way this time). The road I took ran parallel with the trenches, and at this point the Germs were not much more than 60 to 70 yards away. After slackening slightly to turn the corner, I commenced to get up speed (as it is not advisable to waste time in these conditions) when the Bosches sent up a starlight, which fell a few yards behind me.

I was instantly spotted as my handlebars reflected the light, and I was thrown in bold relief. I immediately applied my brakes and threw myself into a ditch and the side of the road and remained whilst the Germs opened a heavy rifle fire in the direction in which I was. I had time to think, and I decided to wait for five or ten minutes in case they should re-commence, and this proved to be the case, for after a pause of some 30 seconds they started again. However they did no harm, and 10 minutes later I mounted and got safely to the farm where I "turned in" on some straw and spent a very comfortable night in spite of the noise as the bullets hit the other side of the stone wall. We left just before daylight and, with the other cyclists, I went to the Signallers' billet and rested again until dinner-time.

23.12.1914

At night we were for the trenches again, and I went to Headquarters which was in the cellars of the Farm I mentioned when I first went to the trenches. Headquarters is where the Commanding Officer and the Adjutant stay, and the Chief Signal Station of the Battalion is there. A wire runs from Battalion Headquarters to Brigade Headquarters, and also lines are laid on in the other direction to each Company in the trench. It is always best to be on Headquarters Signal Station as invariably the Office has been built by the Royal Engineers, fitted with spaces for instruments, and is usually "comfortable". Often Headquarters is in a cellar of a house or farm as in this case, whereas a Station in the trench is an ordinary "dug-out" where perhaps one has to work the "buzzer" lying on one's back, which is by no means conducive to speed or accurate working. My experience in the trenches proves that the Signallers' "dug-outs" are the best, for when one Battalion relieves another the same "dug-out", which in the first place has been chosen for Signalling on account of its being dry and roomy for working purposes, is handed over to the in-coming Signallers, whereas any "dug-out" available the other men have to take and to a certain extent the Signallers worked together to have a good "dug-out".

I was on duty on the trench lines from 5.00pm to 9.00pm and had plenty to do to keep myself occupied. At this time none of the section knew the Morse Code well enough for rapid working and in our spare time we used to practise, for when there are several long messages and one cannot get them through much quicker than six or eight words a minute, it is going to take a considerable time to finish the work. By the time I left the Battalion, we were working at a speed of 20 to 25 words a minute.

With regard to messages, it is not always a case of urgent military matters being wired through, but such as "Tell Mr Blank his breakfast is ready" etc. It is also possible for a person to hand a telegram in at the Signal Office in the trench for an address in London or any part of the world (Germany and her allied countries excluded) paying the prescribed fee, which will be delivered however, with a fair delay, as the message has to go through the Signal Offices of the Battalion, Brigade, Division, Army Corps and other stations before it gets well away from the fighting area.

I had a full night's rest as I had been on duty the night before, and except for a certain amount of artillery activity on the part of the Germs, it was fairly quiet.

24.12.1914

I was on duty again from 8.00am to midday on Thursday the 24th December (Xmas eve) and in the afternoon I crawled behind a hedge and got to some cottages where we had left our cycles, and gave mine a clean-up, which was very necessary. It was a beautiful sunny day, and very clear. There was a factory behind the houses and this could be reached without any great difficulty. It had been badly shelled. A high chimney had been hit, the shell having made a large hole near the top, but otherwise it was sound.

With another man I went to have a look round the factory for "souvenirs" such as shell heads or anything of interest. Of course we should not have been near the place, but it was interesting. Whilst looking at the furnace, my chum,[15] who knew something of factories, mentioned that if we got through the furnace we would be able to go inside the chimney and being a clear day, we might get a view behind the German lines. I suggested that he should lead the way so he crawled through the grate and I followed. We looked up through the chimney and saw the sky, and inside the chimney there were rungs placed at certain intervals, so we commenced climbing with the idea of reaching the shell hole above. My chum went first, and well I knew it, for at every step he took I got a supply of soot and dust. We reached the shell hole, and with a pair of field glasses saw the Germs a mile or so behind the firing line, some working, others walking or cycling, carts with rations or wounded men passing along the roads in rear of their lines. Altogether it was a very interesting experience.

We came down singly so as not to let the one underneath get too much soot, and returned to Headquarters for a wash and brush up, which was very necessary. But we had just got back, when the Germs sent over about a dozen shells near the factory, but they did no damage. Evidently we had been spotted and the Bosches thought that it was an observation station, and every now and again they would send a few shells at the factory, so we were instrumental in wasting the Germs' ammunition. At any rate I hope that we choose for our observation stations cleaner places than this chimney.

Towards evening the Germs became very hilarious, singing and shouting out to us. They said in English that if we did not fire they would not, and eventually it was arranged that shots should not be exchanged. With this they lit fires outside their trench, and sat round and commenced a concert, incidentally singing some English songs to the accompaniment of a bugle band. A Germ officer carrying a lantern came slightly forward and asked to see one of our officers to arrange a truce for tomorrow (Xmas Day).

An officer went out (after we had stood at our posts with rifles loaded in case of treachery) and arrangements were made that between 10.00am and noon, and from 2.00pm to 4.00pm

---

[15] J.M. Dear R.I.P.

tomorrow, intercourse between the Germs and ourselves should take place. It was a beautiful night and a sharp frost set in, and when we awoke in the morning the ground was covered with a white raiment. It was indeed an ideal Christmas, and the spirit of peace and goodwill was very striking in comparison with the hatred and death-dealing of the past few months. One appreciated in a new light the meaning of Christianity, for it certainly was marvellous that such a change in the attitude of the opposing armies could be wrought by an event which happened nigh on 2,000 years ago.

25.12.1914 (Xmas Day)

During the night two men were reported to be missing and I had to go out early in the morning on my cycle to try to find them. I went to the Dressing Station in Chappelle d'Armentières a mile or so away, but they had not been there. Later in the day the Bosches[16] told us that two men the night before had walked into their trench in a state which proved that they had "drunk of the loving cup, not wisely, but too well". We asked that they should be returned to us, but they refused on account of the fact that these men had seen the position of their machine guns. They promised, however, to wire to their Headquarters and see what could be done in the matter. Later we were informed that it had been decided to intern them in a Civilian Camp, and not treat them as prisoners of war, so as this seemed fair and the only course open we left it at that.

At 9.00am as I was off duty I received permission to go to Mass at a Church which I had discovered whilst hunting for the missing men. This Church was terribly shelled, and was within the range of rifle fire, as was clearly proved by the condition of the wall facing the trenches, and no effort had been made to clear the wreckage, as to attempt this would have been fraught with danger. A priest, however, had come in from Armentières to minister to the few people who were still living in the district. In this Church which would hold about 300, there were some 30 people, and I was the only soldier. It was indeed a unique service, and during a short address which the priest gave I was about the only one who was not crying, and that because I did not understand much of what was being said.

---

[16] German account incorrect. See note dated 4th November 1939.

I returned to Headquarters and went on duty from noon to 2.00pm, during which time I partook of my Christmas Fare which consisted of "Bully", "Spuds", Xmas pudding, and vin rouge, which latter we found in one of the cellars on the farm.

In the afternoon I went out and had a chat with "our friends the enemy". Many of the Germs had costumes on which had been taken from the houses nearby, and one facetious fellow had a blouse, skirt, top hat, and umbrella, which grotesque figure caused much merriment. Various souvenirs were exchanged which I managed to send home. We also had an opportunity of seeing the famous Iron Cross which some of the men wore attached to a black and white riband. These crosses are very well made and have an edging of silver. The man's name is engraved on one side, and the reason of the award briefly stated on the other. I have also a number of Germ signatures and addresses on a fly leaf of my "Active Service Pay Book" and it was arranged that at the end of the War we would write one to the other if we came through safely.

The Germs wanted to continue a partial truce until the New Year, for as some of them said, they were heartily sick of the War and did not want to fight, but as we were leaving the trenches early next morning and naturally did not want them to know, we insisted on the truce ending at midnight, at which time our artillery sent over to them four shells of small calibre to let them know that the truce, at which the whole World would wonder, was ended and in its place, death and bloodshed would once more reign supreme.

13. Princess Mary Christmas Card 1914

A SIGNALLER'S WAR

14. King and Queen Christmas Card 1914

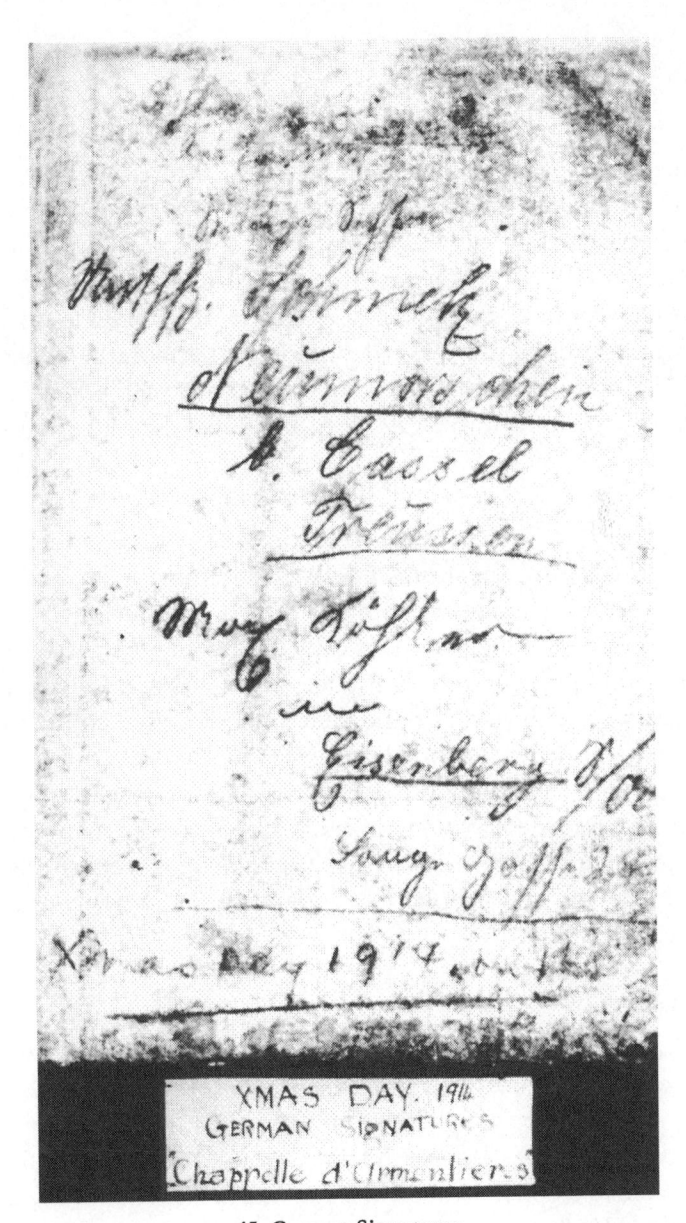

15. German Signatures

26.12.1914

At 4.30am next morning we were relieved in the trenches and marched a distance of three or four miles to Houplines, which proved to be our "home" for the next five months. We were billeted in a flax mill which was not at all comfortable, but just now it was impossible to have a better resting-place.

We had come to Houplines to join the 18th Brigade in the 6th Division, as previously we had only been temporarily attached to the 7th Division. During the day I was on cycling duty, so was unable to make up for the little sleep I had had the night before.

27.12.1914

The next day, Sunday the 27th December, I went to the Church, which, considering the firing line was not more than half a mile away, had not suffered very badly from shells, but being in a hollow was no doubt its safeguard. The Church is alongside the River Lys, which at this point separates France from Belgium. I looked over the narrow breach and for the first time saw the noble country, which has so bravely defended its integrity.

There was a large congregation, for by this time a number of people had returned to their homes, and although many of them were uninhabitable on account of their having been shelled, this small town on the whole had not suffered very considerable damage.

28.12.1914

The next day I managed to arrange with the guard on the bridge to allow me to cross over to Ploegsteert (Belgium) to get some cigars, which were of better quality and cheaper than those obtainable in France. During the day it poured with rain, so I stayed in and we had a concert round the fire which lasted until it was time to get into "Kip".

31.12.1914

During the evening of Thursday the 31st December 1914 we received an invitation from the artillery to a concert which they had arranged to take place behind the guns, and the Battalion accepted it. This concert was quite unique and good, and a few minutes before midnight we sang "Auld Lang Syne" and "God Save the King", and so the Old Year passed out.

What would the New Year bring forth?

CHAPTER 3

France

From 1st January 1915 until 31st May 1915

1.1.1915

Orders were received early this morning, Friday the 1st January 1915, that we were to relieve the Durham Light Infantry in the trenches at night. Our Brigade consisted of the Durham Light Infantry, East Yorks, West Yorks, and Sherwood Foresters - all Regulars - and ourselves a Territorial Unit attached to the Brigade, which system of four Regular Battalions and one Territorial Battalion to a Brigade was in vogue all along the line. It was a very gusty day, and during the afternoon the rain commenced to fall in torrents, and by the time we had reached the trenches (which were knee-deep in water) we were wet through. With two other Signallers I was attached to "A" Company, but there were no lines yet laid on to the Signal Station, so we turned in to our "dug-out", which we had "collared" on account of its size and dryness, and slept through the night.

2.1.1915

Saturday the 2nd January was quite fine and a change from the previous day but the trenches were still full of water. During the morning I made a tour along the length of the line we were holding, and in these pages is a sketch indicating the various points of interest.

The line extended from a Farm which had been badly shelled, and which was therefore designated "Shelled-out Farm" at one end, and the right bank of the River Lys on the other.

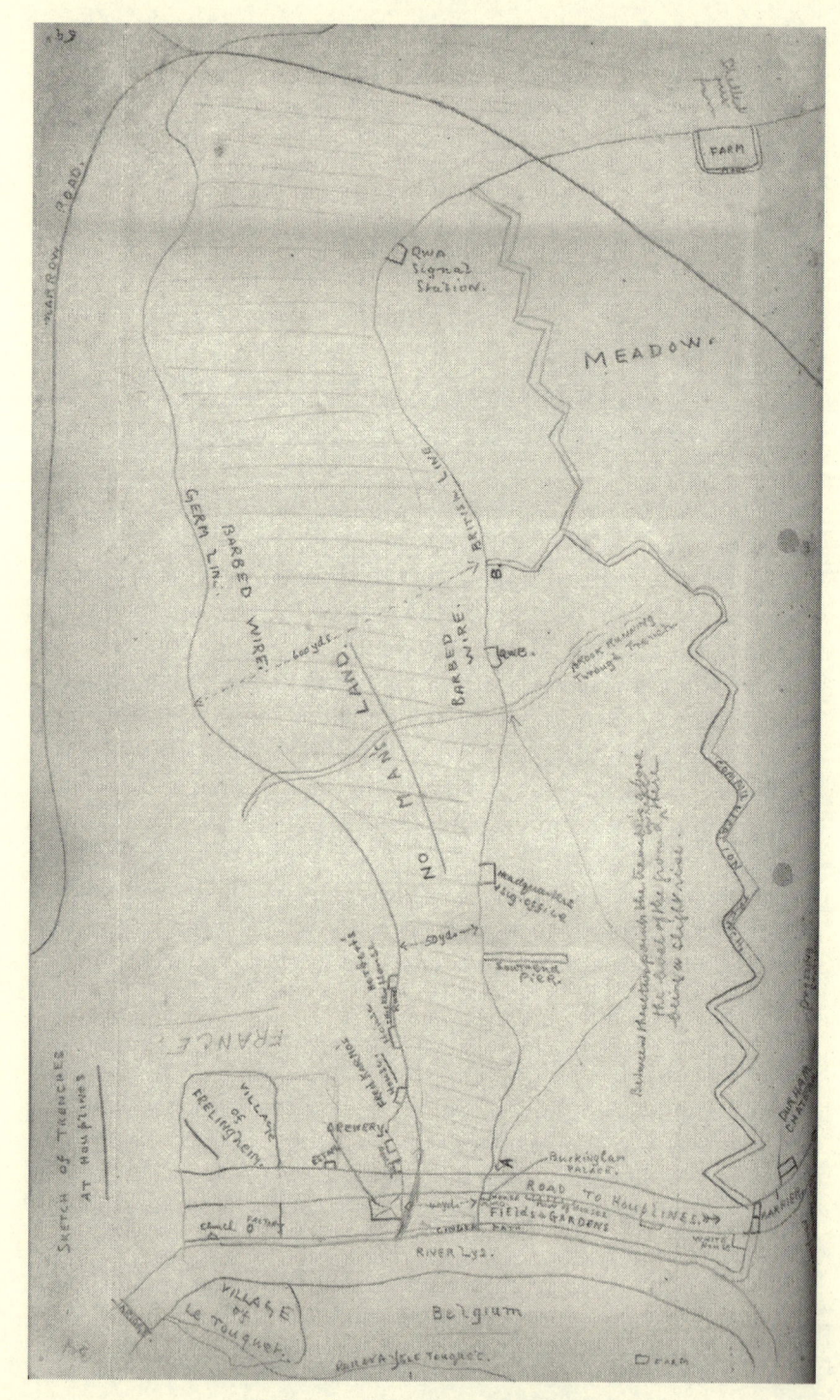

16. Sketch of Trenches at Houplines

Between the river and the road, which ran parallel with the banks, was a cinder path (which when not flooded we used to walk along to the trenches on the left of the road), and a few houses with long gardens. The house nearest the Germ lines was used by our officers for a "dug-out", and named Buckingham Palace, there being a room in the rear which had not been badly damaged. Behind a wall the Signallers had taken an outhouse which proved to be a very comfortable Signal Office. This Station was officially called Q.W.D, but unofficially KYBNOOT KABIN, which being translated is, Keep Your Blooming (?) Nose Out Of This KABIN.

Beside Buckingham Palace there is a yard where the men would come to stretch their legs from the trench which ran right in front of the Palace. The Germ trench was about 35 to 40 yards away. Whilst we were here the Germs did not shell this House, as to do so would mean firing over the village of Frelingheim (which was in their possession) and their own trenches being so near to ours, it was too risky to send shells over in case they hit their own men. But we on the other hand had open ground to fire across, and could put shells into any part of their trench and we used especially to fire heavily at a Brewery, which was said to have accommodation in its cellars for a thousand men. When I first went to these trenches this brewery was practically undamaged, and had a high roof from which the Germs would snipe into our trench. By the time we left however, there was no brewery to be seen, and in its place merely a mass of bricks and wood.

"Buckingham Palace", which was facing this brewery, was brought down by rifle fire making holes in the wall; but this was after a period of four of five months.

In the yard of "Buckingham Palace" there was a pump which, to use from one side was quite safe, but from the other, certain death, as we had illustrated only too well until we discovered that a large portion of the wall which would have made effective cover for the pump, had been cut away by Germ bullets, for they were always firing at this point as they could hear the pump being worked. After a time we had pipes fitted across the road to Headquarters, so that in these trenches there was always a large supply of water. (If used for drinking purposes it had to be boiled.) In fact there was water in abundance, the river having over-ridden its banks and filled the trenches to the road for three months from the time we arrived. The moat round the farm at the other end of our line was also flooded, so plenty of water was there and incidentally in the trenches nearby in consequence. In case even then there was not enough water, in the centre of the line there was a brook which did its utmost to swamp us out, and although it did not quite succeed in its object, it kept a party of men working day and night for three months pumping the water out of the trench. After our first few days in these trenches the field at the back, being slightly below the level of the trench, was flooded, so on the whole we could not complain of shortage of water.

Along the road there was a house with the wall facing the Germs painted white, and at this wall they used to fire quite considerably. After a time we put a quantity of mud in a circle on this wall, providing the Germs with a good target, and incidentally wasting their ammunition.

Further along the road towards Houplines was the Dressing Station, to which the wounded were first taken for attention.

When going into the trenches, one branched off the road by the White House either to the left taking the cinder path, when not flooded, for Buckingham Palace; or to the right across the field to Southend Pier. Perhaps it will not be out of place to give a few other names to the "Dug-outs" and other points in the trench.

    MORSE HOUSE (Q.W.A. Signal Station)
    ST. MARTIN'S LE-GRAND (Headquarters Signal Station)
    KUMINGSUR (Officers' Servants)
    WANDSWORTH PRISON (Miners)
    LATRINE VIEW
    SUMSWANK (Adjutant's "Dug-out")
    LA MAISON VERTE
    THE BLACK CAT
    MAD JACK'S
    HELL'S DELIGHT
    LUDGATE HILL (A rise in the trench)
    WESTMINSTER BRIDGE (planking over brook running through trench)
    FACINE WALK (path behind trench laid with facines)
    SOUTHEND PIER (planking for entering trench near Headquarters)
    BOMB STREET (bombing post)
    CHICKEN RUN (row of outhouses in Germ lines)

FRED KARNO'S (house in Germ lines)
HERBERT'S (house in Germ lines)

There are many other names, which it would perhaps be better not to mention here but they were very funny and descriptive of the position. These names were used when desiring to stipulate any portion of the trench, whether speaking one to the other, or in communication with the artillery. For instance we might report that there were a large number of men working in the trench by the "chicken run" (as could be seen by planks moving above the level of the trench, or water being bailed out) and we would ask them to shell just in front of the "chicken run".

4.1.1915

The weather had become absolutely vile, the rain continuing practically without a break for three days, and on Monday the 4th January, one of the men on Q.W.A. Station with me had an attack of Rheumatism, which caused him to leave the trench, and eventually got him returned to England. We therefore had to carry on with only two men on the station.

6.1.1915

The Germs celebrated the Feast of the Epiphany by shelling the Cemetery in our rear, which by no means improved the atmosphere.

7.1.1915

During the night of the 7th January we had a terrible rain storm, and many "dug-outs" fell in. The trenches were in an awful condition. Fortunately the "dug-out" which we had was very well built, and a fair amount of wood had been used to hold up the earth roof, so that as we sat by our instruments we did not have any rain through the roof, and remained dry. This is one advantage of being a Signaller. Another point to be noted is that a Signaller does no digging, fatigues or any work other than on the wire. In the trenches food is brought in by the Company's fatigue party for the Signallers attached to the Company. In the case of the Signallers attached to Headquarters, their food comes with the rations for the officers and perhaps that accounts for the fact why the Signallers attached to Headquarters get so fat. I have often heard of cases when rations for the officers were missing, and I could give a pretty good guess where they might have been found.

8.1.1915

Early in the morning of Friday the 8th January we had a double tragedy. A corporal had been to get some water a short distance behind the trench (for the pipe was not yet laid from Buckingham Palace) but he had left it rather late, and when he was coming back across the field, it was beginning to get light and about 20 yards from Southend Pier, the Germs saw, fired and hit him.[17] He was seen from our trench, and immediately the Stretcher Bearers were called for and one man went out, but the Germs fired and hit him[18] as he was in the act of bandaging the corporal. Before the order had been received that no other man was to go out, a man[19] from my Company crawled out on his stomach in the mud, and succeeded in reaching these men, but immediately he commenced to dress their wounds the Germs fired, and he had to return. For this attempt he was awarded the Distinguished Conduct Medal. When I went to Headquarters during the afternoon I saw these two men both dead lying in the water (for the field was flooded), the stretcher bearer lying with his arm round the neck of the other man.

Even after dark next night we could not get these men in for a long time as the Germs were firing heavily in their direction in the hope of catching anybody who went out to them.

9.1.1915

The rain continued on Saturday the 9th January, and the trenches were absolutely awful.

The artillery were desirous of shelling a redoubt behind the Germ lines which was being strongly fortified by the enemy, and an officer from the battery came to the trenches to direct the shooting, which he did over the wire from our station. It was very interesting to see the shells burst in different places according to whether the officer wired degrees and minutes to the right or left, increasing and decreasing the range until the object was hit.

---

[17] Corporal Roche.
[18] Rifleman Tibbs.
[19] Rifleman Pouchot D.C.M.

> **THE QUEEN'S WESTMINSTERS.**
>
> **GALLANT WORK OF TERRITORIALS IN THE TRENCHES.**
>
> **THREE D.C.M.s**
>
> No history of the part which the Territorials have played in the first year of the war would be complete without special reference to the fine work of the 1st Battalion Queen's Westminsters (16th County of London), three of whose members have recently been awarded the Distinguished Conduct Medal.
>
> These three are:—
> Sergeant A. G. Fulton, one of the finest rifle shots in the British Empire.
> Corporal J. B. Hill.
> Rifleman J. H. Pouchot.
>
> The "Daily Express" is able to give interesting details of the gallant part played by the Queen's Westminsters, who went to the front in November, and who have the distinction of being under fire for eight months, without rest at a base camp, and of having been among the first Territorial units to be entrusted with the holding of trenches unassisted by the Regulars. This is the fact of which the members of this "crack" Territorial regiment are, perhaps, proudest of all, although their colonel has been made a C.M.G. and their adjutant decorated, while individual riflemen have been mentioned in despatches, five others recommended for distinctions, and many score granted commissions since the outbreak of the war.
>
> **CRAWLING UNDER FIRE.**
>
> The deed which won Rifleman Pouchot the coveted medal is characteristic of the men of the 1st Battalion. Here is the story as told to a "Daily Express" representative on Saturday by a comrade who was present at the time.
>
> "It was Corporal Roche, of the battalion, a prominent Bisley marksman, who began the affair," he said.
>
> "The corporal ventured out one morning from the sort of sand-bag fortification we were holding in order to get water from a stream at the rear. Unfortunately he was seen by the Germans, and shot and mortally wounded.
>
> "One of our stretcher-bearers, seeing him fall, promptly went out to his assistance. He, too, was brought down.
>
> "Then Rifleman Pouchot, who is only seventeen or eighteen years of age—so young that he has been sent back to England—started out to render assistance to his comrades. They lay about sixty yards away, and for half that distance the boy was under fire.
>
> "He crawled this thirty yards or so on his stomach, and crept back again afterwards in the same way. It was a very gallant deed, and by the greatest of good luck Pouchot got back without a scratch."
>
> Another hero of the Queen's Westminsters whose bravery deserves to be placed on record is Sergeant Rogers, of the old "D" Company, who, on Christmas-eve, heard a comrade's shout of "Help!" outside the trenches, and was shot and mortally wounded while going to his assistance.
>
> Much might be written of Sergeant Fulton's exploits; of his "bull's-eye" through a window into a German's body at 300 yards, of his little "sortie" armed with a trenching-tool in company with an officer, and the pair's return with the "bag" of one German killed and two German prisoners.
>
> Only a fortnight ago the Queen's Westminsters were shelled for eighteen hours. At one time their trenches were less than sixty feet from the Germans.

17. Three DCMs for QWR

Unfortunately our men had not got used to being so near as 40 to 50 yards to the Germs, and many a man during these days put his head to the loophole instead of using a periscope, which invariably meant death or at least a wound in the head, for the Germs could see and fire at us from holes in the walls of houses in Frelingheim, and we could not see them. Several casualties were recorded in this manner, and on Saturday the 9th January the first officer to be killed was caught through looking through a loophole at something which a man had seen and reported.

He was my Company Captain[20] and the Officer who had been in charge of the recruits when we first joined the Battalion. He got us to sign our names under his when undertaking Foreign Service, and it was largely due to his remarks and advice that so many men agreed to Imperial Service. He was liked very much by both the officers and men being always ready with a joke, and the Battalion lost a good soldier when he was killed. A Sergeant[21] of the same Company was killed two days previously practically at the same spot, and amongst the men, this part of the trench had a heavy toll.

10.1.1915

Sunday the 10th January opened fine and sunny, but after we had cleaned the trenches and bailed out the water, it commenced to rain, continuing through the night.

11.1.1915

On Monday the 11th January I received a parcel from home containing new under clothing, socks, etc. I put these on and felt nice and dry and desired to keep in this state as long as possible. Unfortunately "duty called" and I had to go along the trench, so rather than get my new things wet, I "paddled" in the way in which the kiddies like to at the seaside. I took off my boots and socks and tucked up my "trucks" and waded through the mud and water, (which was by no means warm), and I kept myself dry to a certain extent - but not for long.

Orders came through that the General had decided to leave the holding of the part of the line opposite the village of Frelingheim entirely to the Westminsters. This was certainly an honour, for it was the most likely portion for an attack as there was the road leading through Houplines to Armentières, and also it was the most dangerous. To do this it was necessary to halve the length of the line we were holding at present, so as to have one half of the Battalion in the trenches and the other half out. The line was therefore cut down to the space between A and B marked in ink on the map.[22]

Every few days the half-battalion out of the trenches would relieve the other, and this would save an amount of confusion and work as every man would know which "dug-outs" to take over, and

---

[20] Captain Shattock.
[21] Sergeant Wilson.
[22] Moon was so bright that it was almost like day.

any portion of the trench to which he might have to go. It also tended to a man working harder to improve his "dug-outs" or portion of the trench, knowing that it was reserved for him next time.

By the time we left Houplines for Ypres these trenches were in splendid condition, with good drainage and "dug-outs" most commodious and comfortable. Of course it meant hard work, but it was worth it. Two companies, one being that to which I was attached, were informed that they would be relieved during the next night, and the other two companies would remain in until relieved by the out-going companies in a few days. (The system of eight companies to the Battalion had been altered to four, i.e. A and B became A; C and D - B; E and F - C; G and H - D).

12.1.1915

At 4.30am on Tuesday the 12th January part of the Sherwood Foresters relieved the two companies, and after handing over the wires to their Signallers, the other man on Q.W.A. Station and I, climbed out of the trenches and went across the fields to the White House on our way encountering much mud, and I am sorry to say my new clothes looked new no longer.

We walked along the road to Houplines and called in at an Estaminet for some "cafe au lait", the proprietor having opened his shop as soon as our men began coming out of the trenches.

When we arrived at Houplines, the Company, who had gone before us, were waiting in the streets arranging billets. As we were tired and did not want to hang about, we went to the house where the Officers' servants were quartered and with whom we were rather chummy, and turned in about 5.30am on the floor with them.

We "got up" about 10.00am, had a good wash and brush up, and breakfast, after which we went to report ourselves in case we were being hunted for. Major Cohen, a senior major to whom we reported, told us that Battalion Headquarters out of the trenches was to be the Chateau de la Rose, and that lines were being laid from the Chateau to Brigade Headquarters in Armentières, and Battalion Headquarters in the trenches and that by tomorrow, we were to move into the Chateau and open up the Signal Station there. As the Q.W.A. Station in the trench was no longer in use for our Battalion, this call would be taken over for the Chateau.

18. Map of Ypres

Later in the morning I cycled to Armentières to get a bath (which was so necessary) as I had heard that there was a convent where one could obtain a hot bath. I found that there were many convents in Armentières and not knowing at which to apply, and feeling that I could not very well knock and ask the nuns, I had to go without.

I did some sight-seeing on my way back, and came across a church, named St. Jean d'Arc, which had been terribly shelled. It was a fine big building with a Norman tower, which although it had been hit several times, had stood the strain. The roofing and sides however, had completely given in. I entered by the door under the tower and looked on a scene of absolute ruination. The only article undamaged was a large crucifix at the bottom of the church. This crucifix was massive and could not be moved easily which no doubt accounts for the fact that everything else had been removed from the church except this crucifix and a few chairs and such articles. Shrapnel had damaged the woodwork of the cross but the figure was in perfect condition. With so much destruction around, it is marvellous that this crucifix was undamaged. I have since seen several other cases of wholesale damage within a few feet of a crucifix, which however had not been touched. For instance in Ypres the Cathedral(which has been practically razed to the ground) stands a large crucifix over the High Altar, undamaged, looking down on the wreckage and ruin of that one time glorious church.

Except for a few houses round this church in Armentières, the district had not been shelled, proving clearly the object of the Germs. I was told by some people who were living nearby that every day, it was bombarded from the 6th to the 28th October 1914 and that on Sundays the Germs shelled it with extra violence. Whether this latter observation is true or the result of a lively imagination, I cannot say, for it is possible that these good people imagined the heavier bombardment on Sundays.

13.1.1915

The next day, Wednesday the 13th January, we moved into the "Chateau de la Rose". The Chateau stands in its own fairly spacious grounds, with the rear bordering on to the River Lys and a few yards away from the Houplines church, which is on the other side of the road. There is a small moat running round the two sides and the front faces the "parc". It had not been damaged by shellfire beyond a few broken windows (shrapnel), which we had repaired before taking up our residence.

For the Signal Office and the sleeping apartments of the Signallers, was fitted up a long oak-panelled room, (facing the river and Belgium) running the whole length of the house from side to side. On the North side of this room opened three doors - the hall, dining room, and a passage to the spiral staircase for some small rooms and the round tower at this end of the house. The other end of the room had two doors - the drawing room, and a passage leading to another spiral staircase for a turret at the south side of the building.

The inhabitants had left their house and gone to Boulogne leaving a "domestic" in charge. Most of the smaller furniture had been removed, but such things as the grand piano, tables, chairs, etc., were still in the house. We opened up the station, and I was on duty from 8.00pm to midnight.

19. Chateau de la Rose, Houplines

14.1.1915

The next day, Thursday the 14th January, I cycled with another Signaller to Armentières and had a bath at the "Convent des Petites Soeurs des Pauvres". There was an Irish sister in the convent and we had a chat with her in our native tongue. After our bath she brought us a cup of hot milk each. We then paid a visit to the chapel, which was very beautiful. The walls and altar were painted white, and were spotlessly clean. The chapel had sustained no damage although buildings nearby including a church had been severely shelled. I went to Confession and Holy Communion in this chapel after my bath. According to the rites of the church, it is not permissible to receive Holy Communion on a day on which food has been taken but a privilege has been granted by the Pope to soldiers who are on active service and in danger, for it is often not possible to receive fasting.

On returning to the Chateau, an artillery duel was in progress, and one or two shells fell in our grounds, and branches hanging over the house were broken, but the Chateau itself was not hit. Our chief object was the brewery at Frelingheim, and the Germs were trying to locate the battery, which was firing from a distance of three to four hundred yards behind the Chateau.

15.1.1915

I took on the duties of cook to the section for a few days, which entailed a full night's rest, and no work on the "buzzer". After cooking breakfast on Friday the 15th January a few of us boarded an old boat, which was in a worn-out condition, and had a row on the river, using the sides of ration boxes for oars. We had continually to bail out the water which was fast coming through the cracks until there was an overflow, and we had quickly to get to land to avoid a "ducking". We were just in time, and watched the sinking of the vessel, which however was not a very tragic sight.

16.1.1915

My birthday on Saturday January the 16th was the next event of importance, the chief item being the "cutting the cake" received from home, which was washed down by the best Malaga which could be obtained from the Estaminet owned by Mesdemoiselles Suzanne et Alice. Perhaps a few words about these two young ladies might not be out of place. They kept a high-class establishment, the rear of which backed onto the grounds of the Chateau, and it was the "Headquarters" of the Signal Service Section. Many a time we had dinner cooked in delightful French fashion and partaken of in a private room, which was reserved for us. Mademoiselle Alice had received a decoration for going into the street under fire when the Germs were driven through Houplines and dragging into her house a wounded soldier lying in the middle of the road, and so saving his life. I often had the pleasure of walking from church with them, during which time I elicited various facts with regard to the occupation of Houplines by the Germs.

The people living in houses nearby had permission to sleep every night in the cellars of this Estaminet as they also did in our Chateau, and at any time when the town was being shelled, shelter was afforded them in these cellars. Suzanne and Alice however, always refused to avail themselves of this shelter, preferring to take the same risk as the soldiers. The Estaminet had been hit by shells several times.

20. Alice, a boy and Suzanne

17.1.1915

At five o'clock on Sunday the 17th January we left for the trenches, and I was detailed for the Station at "Buckingham Palace". The cinder track was flooded, so we walked up the road until we were some 75 yards away from the Germs, and then turned off on to the swamped gardens and waded for the rest of the journey, arriving in a somewhat wet condition.

18.1.1915

Doing the usual duty on the instrument, six hours on and six off, the night passed fairly quietly, and the next day was peculiar by having rain, snow, and brilliant sunshine at various intervals. A cat behind our lines occasioned much amusement to the Germs, who fired at it. It is said that a cat has nine lives, evidently this cat had already had eight.

Our water supply was greatly increased by heaven during the next few days, and the flooding of the trench at one part was so bad that it had to be evacuated, and "Buckingham Palace" was cut off from the rest of the Battalion, the only communication being over the wire.

22.1.1915

The Casualties had been mounting up although the past few days had been fairly quiet. Early in the morning of Friday the 22nd January a relief was being carried out for "C" Company who had been in the trench for three weeks, which in our part of the line proved to be the record for some time past (a very unhappy distinction for the sufferers) when a man was hit. We wired at once for the Stretcher Bearers and could plainly hear the man groaning. This was very unsafe for the companies coming into the trenches for it would indicate to the Germs, who could also hear, that there were men moving about. The men therefore got quickly into the trench at any point and were just in time, for the Germs evidently called a "stand-to" and opened rapid fire all along our front. However, a miss is as good as a mile.

The outgoing Signallers were relieved in the evening (for we were not necessarily relieved with the companies), and on my way out I slipped over the bank, and had a short rest in the ditch, getting "some" wet. A bath next morning, however, put me right in this direction.

26.1.1915

On Tuesday the 26th January, I had a good look round the church at Houplines and noticed that the altar rails and confessional had been "gnawed" away. I made enquiries at a local Estaminet at which I had occasion to call, and learned that the Germs, when occupying Houplines, had billeted horses in the church, with this result.

Much enjoyment was provided for the children of the district by an incident, which I witnessed during the afternoon. To prevent the Germs conveying messages by sending them along the river with the tide, an order was issued to the guard on the bridge that all bottles, tins, etc. were to be fired at, and sunk. The youngsters gathered round and watched the water spurt up as the bullets hit the surface. It was quite surprising the number of bottles there were in the water, coming with the tide as many as half-a-dozen at a time. Walking along the bank I discovered the reason.

Round the bend of the river was a brewery, which had been evacuated and left behind was all the equipment of the trade. Large stacks of bottles were in the yard, and the youngsters were busy getting and throwing them into the water. I watched for a time and these children were "relieved" by others from the bridge, to take their turn at watching the shooting and pointing out to the Sentry when they sighted the bottles coming along. This state of affairs went on for about a month or two when it was thought advisable to get a net to stretch right across the river. The sentries seemed to miss not having bottles to fire at, and this net certainly upset the plans of the youngsters who no doubt turned their ingenuity into other directions and caused more mischief.

27.1.1915

Wednesday the 27th January, the Kaiser's birthday, we expected some excitement to relieve the monotony. In the evening I was due for the trenches again, but we had no fun. It had been a lovely day, and the night was very bright, and dangerous for relieving troops. But the moon shone brightly on the flooded fields, and they looked like mirrors, reflecting the light so that it was almost as bright as day. We had to go in singly, as it was less likely that the Germs would see one man than a party. All the same, we had several casualties.

28.1.1915

Snow, rain, and frost was the order for the next day, but in spite of the elements a very lively time was experienced on the other side of the river (Belgium).

30.1.1915

We had a report over the wire on Saturday the 30th January informing us that our aerial service had spotted a column of the enemy approaching from Lille, so we expected that something was going to happen, but nothing unusual took place until the following day Sunday the 31st January, when the Germs bombarded Houplines heavily with the result - one young girl killed.

France, 22/1/15

Dear Ma,

Sorry to hear from Edie's letter that Mr Webb is queer. I hope that by now he is much better. How are the two boys Anscombe?

It may possibly interest you to know how we are grubbing, so I will give you my yesterday's menu. I won't say that it is always as good, but on the whole we have something after this style.

Brekker. Soup (made from packets)
        Ham & Buttered Toast & Cocoa

Lunch. Salmon (gift of the government of British Columbia)
        & Bread & Butter.

Dinner. Mutton, Ham, Potatoes mashed in butter. & Tea.

Tea   Cocoa & Cake.

During meals peppermints, Chocolate Cheroots (small cigars) & for supper we only had a couple of slices of cake & chocolate.

There are two of us & we work together, one on duty & the other cooking. We also share our parcels etc together.

21. Some Diet!

The month finished with a heavy fall of snow.

1.2.1915

Monday the 1st February opened bright and fine. During the night the artillery on either side had been very active, and in the morning we took the opportunity of the fine weather to shell the brewery with our heavy guns. From a small hole in the wall of "Buckingham Palace" I watched the shells bursting in the brewery, a matter of about 40 yards' distance. The shooting was splendid, the object being hit every time. The roof gave way and fell in; great masses of masonry tumbled into the Germ trenches; wood, iron, bricks, etc. flew upwards to a great height, many pieces of which fell into our own trench.

After the shelling had ceased and the smoke and dust fanned away by the passing breeze, the change we saw wrought by some dozen shells was marvellous. The one-time presentable building was now no more than a heap of ruins, but in spite of this the great point was whether we had reached the cellars.

A draft of 250 men arrived from England to replace our casualties and they did not choose a good day for getting near the firing line, for it was what is called a "lively" day and an anxious period, as we were expecting an attack, the shelling having been so violent. This night I was relieved from the trenches.

2.2.1915

Our artillery had reported that from observations made, there were no civilians in Frelingheim but the following day, Tuesday the 22nd February, we were told that a large number of French prisoners had been brought up during the night and were clearing the wreckage behind the brewery and some houses to which our shells had set fire. We therefore did not fire in that direction. These men, our artillery informed us, were quartered in a school which had suffered considerably from our guns on account of the fact that the Germs kept stores there, but we did not shell it again until the "civvies" had left. The question remains, whether the Germs quartered them there hoping that we would shell. I would not like to say.

General Congreave, VC, inspected our draft in the Chateau grounds to-day and made a short speech telling the men not to believe all the tales they had heard, such as one which was prevalent at that time that the Germs were not good shots with the rifle. He said that if they did not believe him they could prove it for themselves by putting their heads above the parapet in our part of the line. He advised them, however, to take his word.

3.2.1915

Whilst on duty on the wire at the Chateau during the afternoon of Wednesday the 3rd February, the Germs sent over a good many shells within 20 or 30 yards from our "home". One fell in the grounds on the path by the entrance door, but fortunately did not burst. The detonator being set showed the distance from which it had been fired, and we passed this information to our battery who gave the Germs a "hot" time, and knowing the range possibly found the Germ battery.

Another shell fell and burst on the towpath of the river and broke our wires. When things quietened down slightly I went out, mended the wires, and brought in some shrapnel bullets as "souvenirs".

4.2.1915

At 7.00pm on Thursday the 4th February, the Germs attacked very violently after a three-quarter of an hour's bombardment, a mile or so to our left, but they were repulsed. We were all "standing to" and in readiness, the men out of the trenches having filled the reserve "trench" (ditch). The noise of the enemy's and our guns was terrific, and the sky was lit up continuously, indicating the large number of shells fired. However, it quietened down after a couple of hours, and we were able to turn in.

I have indicated the general monotony of trench life, and after this I will only state briefly incidents worth recording. Trench work consists of digging, guards, fatigues, with casualties, expectations, realisations (oft times so terrible), wet, cold, shortage of food, and many other discomforts. A Signaller has continuous duty on the telegraph instrument, with all the discomforts except the first three.

7.2.1915

On Sunday the 7th February we fired some grenades from the yard in "Buckingham Palace" (which I had re-entered yesterday without anything special taking place) but as we were not yet initiated in the art of using them, they did not explode on reaching their destination in or near the Germs' trench.

8.2.1915

Monday, the 8th February saw the return of the grenades which we had fired, and this time they did explode, but no damage was done but they hit the roofing of the Palace and brought down to the ground a rafter from the roof, which I promptly collared and chopped up as we were very short of firewood. I am afraid our officers were not pleased with the Signallers on this day, as we had a fire, and they did not on account of a shortage of wood. What we had over we gave to our friends along the trench.

13.2.1915

On Saturday the 13th February, I cycled to Armentières (having come out of the trenches on Thursday) and had a much-needed bath at the convent, received Holy Communion, and "served" at Benediction in the afternoon.

16.2.1915

On Tuesday the 16th February, I was again due for the trenches, so in the afternoon, to prepare ourselves a few of the section went to a concert in Armentières given by a company named "The Follies". This party was composed of officers and men of various regiments who were, or had been, professional artistes, and two Belgian girls and so as to give the soldiers some pleasure when out of the trenches, they were detailed to give a high-class entertainment twice daily at the local theatre, instead of doing trench work. They wore a pierrot's costume, and half-a-franc was the charge for a jolly and bright concert. From generals to "Tommies" patronised these concerts and every effort was made to get the latest London songs and jokes.

We enjoyed the concert immensely, and walked back to Houplines and prepared for the trenches. We had practically forgotten that "there was a War on", but on getting near the trenches we were reminded very vividly that there was. In fact the Signal Section had a narrow escape from being "wiped out".

The previous day had seen much rain, and to avoid going over the swamped fields we decided to walk down the road up to the front trench; other men and fatigue parties were doing the same and they would now and then rest awhile and perhaps place on the ground, not too gently, a tin of tea or anything they might be carrying; for by this time we were hardened to danger and took great risks for the sake of personal comfort.

As we were getting near, a man at the rear stumbled, and made a fearful noise by dropping his rifle and other things he was carrying. The Germs a few seconds later sent up a star shell, which fell on the road some distance behind us, and lit up very brilliantly a large area. There were quite a number of men on the road, and they showed up distinctly. Each man threw himself into the ditch on either side and the Germs opened rapid fire straight down the road, and as there was very little cover even in the ditches, we had to "chance our luck" as to whether we got hit of not. The tin of tea which had been left in the middle of the road reflected like a heliograph from the star shell, and the Germs riddled it with bullets. When the firing had died down somewhat, we made a dash for the trench and just succeeded in gaining our object when the Germs re-commenced.

17.2.1915

Ash Wednesday, the 17th February, wept bitterly, and the river rose to such a degree that we were again flooded out.

18.2.1915

Thursday, however, was quite a nice day, and the Commandant of one of our armoured trains decided to have another "go" at the Frelingheim brewery. There is no doubt about it, we did not want that brewery to adorn the country-side, but joking apart, we wanted to be certain that the cellars were smashed in preparation for an attack on Frelingheim which we were contemplating.

The armoured train carried some heavy pieces which had lately arrived from England, and a significant message to the following effect was received:

"Armoured train bombarding Frelingheim brewery at 2.30pm, sometimes shooting inaccurate so be well down in the trenches and pray all the time".

Considering the fact that the gun was firing from Erquinghem (about 4 miles per crow) and our trench was so near the brewery, we did not quite like the idea, for it is quite reasonable that the shell might fall 40 or 50 yards short in such a long distance, and it would not be a big technical error.

However, we moved from behind "Buckingham Palace" into an officer's "dug-out", and the officer[23] entertained us with some yarns about the South Africa campaign, some of which were not of the drawing-room character. We did not watch the shelling, but the noise of the bursts was ear splitting, and great lumps of "brewery" were driven into our trench, embedding themselves in the mud. During the evening a Company of the Canadian Highlanders who were attached to our Battalion came into the trenches for 24 hours for the first time, and we had to "show them the ropes".

20.2.1915

I had been in the trenches in conditions of torrential rain, drizzle, snow, fog and mist and on Saturday the 20th February 1915 a thunderstorm was experienced. In my opinion the noise of thunder, whether near at hand and loud; or distant and rumbling, is not like the bursting of shells as so many writers indicate, but it is quite distinct from the short sharp explosion of a bursting shell. A considerable amount of rifle or machine gun fire at a distance of about half a mile resembles very accurately the noise of rumbling thunder.

21.2.1915

On Sunday, the 21st February, it was very misty during the morning, and the guards were doubled, for it was a good opportunity for a local attack, but towards mid-day it cleared, and finished up a beautiful day. In the evening I came out of the trenches and was on duty at the Chateau from 11.00pm until 1.00am on Monday the 22nd.

23.2.1915

On Tuesday the 23rd February, I went with a chum for a walk into Belgium and crossed the river into France by a boat, which the

---

[23] Captain Lambert.

Royal Engineers provided. The R.Es were reconstructing a bridge, which had some months before been blown up after crossing by the Germs.

24.2.1915

Some more Canadian Highlanders came into our trenches for 24 hours on Wednesday the 24th February, and they had their first experience of trench life amid snow.

26.2.1915

Friday, the 26th February, I went to the trenches for duty at Headquarters Station. It was a very light night, beautiful but dangerous, and one half-company of some 100 men had nine casualties in as many minutes, whilst crossing the flooded fields to the front line.

27.2.1915

Whilst I had been out of the trenches the Durham Light Infantry had commenced mining operations and the next day, Saturday, the 27th February, I went down one of the mines as far as they had bored. It takes months to dig a mine and if the distance between the trenches is considerable it is useless taking the trouble unless a very important object is in view.

A mine is laid in this manner. Three or four tunnels are bored at right-angles to the trench for a distance of about 20 yards (this varies according to the distance of the enemy's trench) and then the heads of these saps are connected by boring to the right and left, parallel with the trench, to prevent the enemy boring past you, and also to provide a listening gallery should the enemy be also mining. If sounds of digging are heard and it is certain that counter-mining is taking place, this gallery would be fired and so stop all operations. The mine is lined with wood, and mud and water is brought out of the mine on trolleys which are pulled along by ropes. Machinery worked by hand provides fresh air for the men working in the mine. The depth underground would be from 15 to 20 feet.

Our object was to get past the Germs' trench and blow up certain buildings in Frelingheim, but we left before this operation had taken place, and I do not know the result of all the work done. Months, sometimes, are spent mining and through miscalculation or unforeseen circumstances the mine, when fired, causes little or no damage, but at other times many men can be put out of action and trenches captured by this method of warfare.

28.2.1915

A large factory chimney had been the cause of a considerable number of our casualties. It had been hit by a small shell, which made a hole near the top, from which the Germs would occasionally fire at us. We had reported this matter and on Sunday the 28th February, our "heavies" informed us that they were going to "try their luck" and see if they could remove this obstacle. These guns were from four to five miles away behind Erquinghem and of course could not see the object at which they were firing. The shooting was directed by an artillery officer from the observation post. The shells fired were I was informed, the "9.2s", and weighed 240 pounds.

The first shell went some 30 yards to the left of the chimney. The second shot went too much to the right, but the third caught the chimney a few feet from the bottom and it fell to the ground raising a great amount of dust. The Germs greatly objected to our demonstrating our satisfaction by cheering, and opened rapid rifle fire and we kept low in the trench until they had finished their "hate".

I was on duty in the evening, and the second month of 1915 drew to a close with me sitting in my "dug-out" on a ration box, smoking a pipe, with my instrument by my side and wondering when I would see home again.

1.3.1915

Monday the 1st March 1915, opened fine, and much artillery was in vogue on either side. In the afternoon there was a thunderstorm. The evening was very brilliant and the Germs entertained us with selections on a bugle. Music under such conditions is rather peculiar. The bugler would play a tune right through, and the Germs would sing to it and if it was a tune we knew (for they played several English songs) we also sang. Whilst the music was in progress neither side fired, but, as applause, each man fired a few rounds from his rifle to which the Germs replied. After this "applause" the music would start again and again no firing. After a couple of hours of this the Germs shouted "finished" and both sides cheered the bugler lustily.

3.3.1915

I came out of the trenches in the evening of Wednesday the 3rd March.

4.3.1915

On Thursday the 4th March with a Signaller from the 18th Brigade I cycled to Armentières and as I had heard much about a village, by name Bois Grenier, which had been completely wrecked by shellfire, I suggested that we should go and have a look at it. We therefore cycled through Chappelle d'Armentières, L'Armée and Griespot arriving at Bois Grenier about noon. Our front line ran about 20 yards in front of Bois Grenier and to get there one had to go down a road, which was under rifle fire and could be seen by the Germs. It was however hedged on either side but by keeping low and riding fast we anticipated that we would not be spotted. Of course we were not allowed to come down this road or to go to the village in daytime. Just before we arrived the Germs had been shelling the village and set fire to some cottages, which were blazing away merrily.

Up to this time I had not seen such havoc and destruction and I was greatly struck by the air of desolation. Not a soul in sight, and nothing but wreckage and ruin could be seen. The church, which at one time had been used as a hospital, was one pile of bricks and there was hardly a house with the upper storey still standing.

I must say this first insight of wholesale destruction made me feel very miserable, for one could not help thinking of the homes broken up and the misery involved, and I did not feel any happier until I had partaken of a large portion of steak and chips with a certain amount of red wine in a cosy Estaminet in Armentières.

In the afternoon we paid a visit to the "Follies".[24]

5.3.1915

The Westminsters had a good concert in a school (which had been shelled) in the evening of Friday 5th March 1915.

---

[24] And then I was for the trenches again. This from memory.

6.3.1915

One grenade fired by the Germs the next day caused eight casualties.

8.3.1915

Both the British and Germs' gunners tried to put some of us "out" on Wednesday the 8th March, the Germs by shelling the Chateau grounds during the afternoon and our own battery dropping a few shells into our trenches in the evening just after I had re-entered the firing line for duty.

10.3.1915

About 3.00am on Wednesday the 10th March we were called up to give the Germs a lively time as an attack was being made at Neuve Chappelle.

Our men did a considerable amount of rifle firing, the reason being to make the Germs think that we were going to attack and thus prevent their moving troops from this district to where the attack was actually in progress. We heard the guns and watched the brilliant flashes, which reflected beautifully against the low clouds causing a variety of colours. During the day we kept up continual firing, and the evening was a relief as things were quieter.

The noise of continued firing is very trying and causes violent headaches, and the smoke of the powder from bursting shells and bullets being fired adds greatly to the uncomfortable pains in the head.

12.3.1915

We were very unkind to the Germs on Friday the 12th March, by repeating an early morning attack, and this time capturing the village of L'Epinette a distance of two or three miles on our right. Again we gave our assistance by opening fire just as the morning light appeared, and this time the Germs got a "severe wind up", sending up flares by the score.

The Signaller on duty with me was wounded early in the day and I had to continue on duty from 2.00am until 10.00pm - a matter of 20 hours without rest. To add to this the Headquarters wire of the Durham Light Infantry had been broken by a bullet and all their messages had to come through my station.

Unfortunately overtime is not allowed in the Army, but surely a shilling a day is good enough pay, and if one gets "knocked out", what does it matter how much money one has received?

14.3.1915

On Sunday the 14th March 1915 we received a wire telling us to prepare to move to Fleurbaix, a distance of some 20 miles from Houplines. Our officers went to inspect the new portion of line, and "packing up" was well in hand when the order was "washed out". Good resulted from this however, as many farewells had to be drunk, and the receipts of the local Estaminet thereby increased.

GERMAN HIGH EXPLOSIVE SHELLS BURSTING NEAR THE ALLIES' TRENCHES.

22. Shell Near Allies' Trenches

After church, I went with a chum to the 43rd Battery and had a close inspection of our 4.5 Howitzer gun and its various parts, including a very marvellous and delicate sighting arrangement. A few rounds were fired whilst we were there which enabled us to see the height to which a howitzer shell can go. When standing behind one of these guns it is possible for an instant to see the shell in the air, looking like a black speck. Unless directly behind the gun one never sees a shell in progress - it is travelling at such a great speed. A good idea of the rate of moving can perhaps be gathered when one takes into consideration that some shells weigh nearly one ton, and to keep such a weight in the air against gravity must require a terrific speed.

Whilst this gunnery was going on the Germs sent over a few shells hoping to find the battery, and on our returning to Houplines, we were informed that one of the Germ's shells had fallen in a large room where there were a number of men, killing seven and wounding about 30, and we saw the men being transferred on stretchers to the Dressing Station.

15.3.1915

Monday the 15th March was a bright clear day and I accepted an invitation of some artillery Signallers to go to the artillery observation post[25] (the position of which, for obvious reasons, I must refrain from stating), and with the aid of a powerful telescope managed to see many objects of interest. The Observation Station was very tall, and one could see over obstacles, and watch men working both in our, and the Germs' trenches.

We were shelling the Germs' position and it was very interesting to watch the result of the explosion of the shells, whilst an officer corrected the range. There was a large Germ working party about 800 yards behind their line, and we were able to scatter them, leaving a few on the ground.

By this time the Germs had commenced defensive operations, and through the scope I counted no less than eight lines of trenches, with a great thickness of barbed wire in front, which shows what a big task it is to advance any long distance.

Carts, cycles, ambulances etc. were moving behind the Germs lines and on my enquiring why we permitted this, I was informed that it was not worthwhile wasting a shell in the hope of catching one or two men, and another reason was that we could not afford to use the shells. This did not make me feel too comfortable, as an infantryman likes to think that the artillery has plenty of

---

[25] Mairie 1922.

ammunition to "back him up" in the event of trouble. Thank goodness that this state of affairs has now been altered.

In the evening I repaired the wire in the reserve trench connecting us with the mountain battery.

19.3.1915

We received a very interesting message whilst in the trenches on Friday 19th March (I had re-entered last night) the text of which is as follows:

"You will be pleased to know that the Germs call the portion of line in front of your gallant Battalion, the "place of death", and they don't like being there at all, Paley (Brigade Major)".

This information - which also appeared in the London papers - was obtained from a prisoner but I think that it must have been due to the accuracy of the artillery fire more than to our work with the rifle, as it was not possible for us to do much on account of the positions taken up in the houses by the Germs.

20.3.1915

The next day, Saturday the 20th March, we spotted a dead Germ between the lines. He had evidently been on patrol overnight and been hit. The Germs left him there for several days before they fetched him in. "Buckingham Palace" suffered severely from grenades today, but upon our replying by shelling, the Germs "gave over".

22.3.1915

We heard of the fall of PRZEMZYL on Monday, the 22nd March and made it the occasion of a demonstration by sending up star shells and cheering, thus "putting the wind up" the Germs.

23.3.1915

At 3.00am on Tuesday the 23rd March, a general "stand to" was called, over the wire, by Brigade. The idea was to see if everything was ready in the event of an attack being made upon us. The message received was to the effect that we were to be ready to repel an attack at once. The reserves were called up to fill the second line of trenches, and the gunners were ordered to fire a number of shells. It was a good test, and everything was done smartly, for as a matter of fact we did not know but that information had been received that the Germs were about to attack us. In the evening I came out of the trenches. It was pouring with rain, and I was not sorry to get to the Chateau to dry my clothes.

27.3.1915

After having a walk into Belgium on Saturday the 27th March, half a dozen Signallers "challenged" the rest of Houplines to a football match. It was a great game, especially as many of the "Froggies" did not know the rules, and as the time went on all the younger generation joined in, and we had the utmost difficulty not to fall over them. We finished the day with a lively discussion round the fire in our room.

28.3.1915

Palm Sunday, the 28th March, was an ideal and cloudless day. Aeroplanes were very busy in consequence, and on account of the blueness of the atmosphere, one could see the full effect of the shells bursting round the machines. The blessing of the "Palms" at church was rather unique, owing to palms not being obtainable, and evergreens, which the congregation brought with them, substituted.

The evening saw me back in the trenches,[26] which were reached without undue excitement. The weather continued fine, and artillery was very active, especially our "heavies" which were continually bombarding Frelingheim. We were informed that our sappers had discovered that the Germs were counter-mining, and that we might have to blow up our own saps, or be blown up ourselves, which was not too pleasant to know. This counter-mining was only taking place in one portion of our line, so we continued working on the other.

30.3.1915

My chum on the Signal Station at "Buckingham Palace" with me had been queer with an attack of influenza, and on Tuesday the 30th March I managed to catch it, and had to come out of the trenches and go to the Dressing Station. If one is queer, I can assure anybody who might think otherwise, that a trench is not the

---

[26] There was only the front line in 1914 and early 1915. A second line dug later was only manned if an attack was likely.

most comfortable place in which to be. I saw the doctor and received some "number nines" (an infallible remedy given by military doctors for all illnesses), and "turned in" on the floor to try and sleep through the night.

I believe I mentioned that the Dressing Station is the first aid post, and is a house about eight hundred yards behind the firing line, so necessarily the accommodation is by no means perfect. The food, however, is of a superior quality and it is a treat to get a hot meal.

1.4.1915 and 2.4.1915

I began to mend on Thursday the 1st April and was feeling very "fed up" at being kept in a room like a caged lion, so on Good Friday, the 2nd April, I told the doctor that I was better and he let me go to the Chateau as there was an empty room in which I could sleep. This permitted me to have some of my chums with me (for it will be remembered that when one half of the section is in the trenches, the other half is out). Orders were received that I was not to go to the trenches until I was quite better to prevent spreading any illness, and I did not complain by any means. In the afternoon Mademoiselle Suzanne took my photo in the Chateau grounds.

23. Author in Chateau Grounds

3.4.1915

I cannot say whether this latter event affected me in any way, but I had a very bad night, and when I went to the doctor the next morning Saturday the 3rd April, he said "Damn me if you haven't got it again", so I had to have more "Number Nines".

4.4.1915

Easter Sunday, the 4th April, I did not enjoy as I was feeling so queer. I went to church however, in the morning, so no doubt I was better spiritually, if not bodily.

5.4.1915

Our motto for Easter Monday, the 5th April, was "business as usual", and our artillery carried out this principle to the letter, and the Germs had a very rough time. I was feeling much brighter, and went for a walk into Belgium with a chum.

6.4.1915

Tuesday the 6th April, I had a look at some "eighteen pounders" (quick firing field gun), and a new anti-aircraft gun on a motor lorry which had lately been attached to our Brigade.

7.4.1915

I was due for the trenches again on Wednesday the 7th April, but the doctor would not let me return, and I was quite satisfied to abide by his decision. In the afternoon with two of my chums I went for a stroll into Belgium.

8.4.1915

Much excitement was occasioned in Houplines on Thursday the 8th April by the Germs shelling the town with a new gun, the shells being of the "coal-box" variety and having a very loud burst. This was our first experience of very big shells as Houplines had lately only had shells of a smaller calibre fired into the town. With several others I went out into the street to watch the effect and we saw a shell go through the roof of the house at the end of the road and burst sending into the road a large amount of household furniture, belongings and bricks.

24. Signal

Several of our windows were broken but the Chateau luckily was not hit. After a couple of hours of this and our guns trying to find the new battery, the shelling died down and we went round examining the size of the shell holes, and some of the holes made by shells falling on soft ground would comfortably accommodate four motor buses and were nearly as deep as the height of the bus.

The effect of this bombardment was that during the next few days a large number of the inhabitants applied for permits to go to a safer place - a very wise procedure.

25. Houplines Church after First Shelling

9.4.1915

Early next morning, Friday the 9th April, the Germs attacked on our right and left and the amount of artillery fire was enormous. In case the noise of the guns was not sufficient it was augmented by a thunderstorm which commenced almost as soon as the guns.

As the Germs were counter-mining we had to blow up one of our saps today, but little or no damage was the result of all the labour spent in digging. The Germs got a certain amount of "wind up" over this operation and consequently commenced firing heavily causing several casualties amongst our men.

11.4.1915

A Germ aeroplane hovered over Houplines about six o'clock on Sunday evening the 11th April, and our anti-aircraft gun succeeded in hitting it, but the machine was not very severely damaged. The plane was high in the sky and as we saw it "topple" the result of it being hit, a hearty cheer was raised and the aeroplane began to descend rapidly. The airman however managed to right the machine and glided down behind his own line and our gunners tried to complete their good work, but the machine managed to escape without again being hit.

12.4.1915

I went to the trenches next day Monday the 12th April and except for a considerable amount of artillery activity nothing of consequence took place.

16.4.1915

A great deal of digging was ordered on Friday the 16th April and we were told later that an attack was to be carried out by the Westminsters against the village of Frelingheim. Many rumours started and it was stated that the General had said that he would not trust any other Battalion with the work. It was only fair that if an attack were made that we should carry it out, as we had solely been holding this part of the line and our men were getting anxious to try conclusions with the Germs and wanted to get into the village, which for so long we had been facing.[27]

Every evening as dusk began to fall large working parties of the Royal Engineers and the regiments in our Brigade started digging and after a month a maze of trenches beautifully made were in evidence. Several communication trenches were made, some wide enough to bring up a small gun undercover, one running through the Chateau grounds from the trench. This trench of course was not used as the width made it dangerous, but if an attack were successful the guns would advance this way instead of using the road. The number of trenches behind the front line would permit a large quantity of troops to be in readiness with comparative safety.

Of course the Germs noticed this work and firing at night increased considerably and our casualty list mounted proportionately. No work was done in these new trenches during the day, but the Germs would shell them and to a certain extent do damage, which would have to be repaired; and Houplines was very severely shelled as a means of the Germs' revenge.

---

[27] Houplines is on the main road to Calais.

17.4.1915

On a Saturday evening, the 17th April, I came out by a new communication trench and bought some stores, including oranges, eggs and pork chops for tomorrow's dinner. I came back with some of the Signallers - and there was a big attack being launched at Ypres where the British took Hill 60, and we could see the reflection of the guns which made very vivid colours in the sky.

We got a message about 11.00pm stating that we had captured the position after exploding mines and we had suffered few casualties. We were also informed that we had forced a Germ aeroplane to the ground and captured the machine and pilot.

18.4.1915

Sunday the 18th April, was an ideal day with plenty of artillery to remind us that there was a War on. The fighting up North continued during the day and increased in violence towards the evening.

19.4.1915

On Monday the 19th April, the Germs shelled the Church at La Bizet (just across the river in Belgium), for although it had been greatly damaged the walls were still standing and I suppose the Germs objected to this.

22.4.1915

A Germ shell set fire to a large farm in Belgium and it was indeed a sight to watch the effect. There was a large quantity of hay and straw for the Army horses kept at this farm and once the fire got a good hold the flames amounted to a great height and dense masses of smoke rolled heavenwards.

During the afternoon some of the Signallers at the Chateau were hunting for "spuds" in the kitchen garden when they came across a couple of beer barrels buried in the ground. Upon opening these barrels they disclosed large quantities of gold and silver plates, the owner of the Chateau evidently burying these goods before quitting his house. We sent all the articles to the Bank of France where no doubt they will be safer.

In the evening I came out of the trenches after a period of 10 days.

23.4.1915

On St George's Day, Friday the 23rd April, I was on duty from 4.00am to 8.00am and later on had a much-needed bath, some bath! The Germs attacked at Ypres using gas and thereby succeeded in driving back the French. We received a message a couple of days later:

"Germs succeeded at Ypres through asphyxiating gas making the French think the devil was playing some tricks and the French bolted aaa The Canadians stood ground".

27.4.1915

On Tuesday the 27th April I returned to the trenches through a new communication trench, which was beautifully made. This communication trench was very useful, for it permitted the Signaller off duty to go out to Houplines and have a meal when feeling so inclined. I need hardly say that no authority was given for this procedure.

28.4.1915

On Wednesday the 28th April, as some changes were taking place in the British line, the half-battalion out of the trenches had orders to go into the trenches across the river; so for the first time the Westminsters held the line in Belgium.

I came out of the trenches at 5.00pm for three hours and managed to get some eatables.

1.5.1915

On Saturday the 1st May the Battalion was relieved under a new arrangement. With another Signaller I was detailed for Signalling duty with the Royal Engineers (1st London Field Company) who were near Erquinghem and we came out of the trenches at 2.30pm.

It was terribly hot and we did not quite know where to find the engineers, and with full pack, rifle and equipment, started to march. We had not gone far when the post cart came along and we managed to get a lift as far as Armentières. We marched from there and eventually found the Royal Engineers at 5.00pm and had a welcome cup of tea.

As I have already mentioned, Erquinghem is some two or three miles from the firing line, and the engineers are very busy here

A SIGNALLER'S WAR

making trench-boards, parapet protectors, sand bags etc.; and a large number of French people, men and women, are also employed. So far Germs' shells had not found their way here, so we reckoned on a nice quiet time.

2.5.1915

I was on duty from 2.00am to 8.00am on Sunday the 2nd May after which I went to Mass at the Cathedral in Armentières. In the evening I had a trip up the river on a pontoon boat to Erquinghem.

3.5.1915

I was on duty from 8.00am until 11.00am and I then cycled to Houplines to get any letters there might be for us.

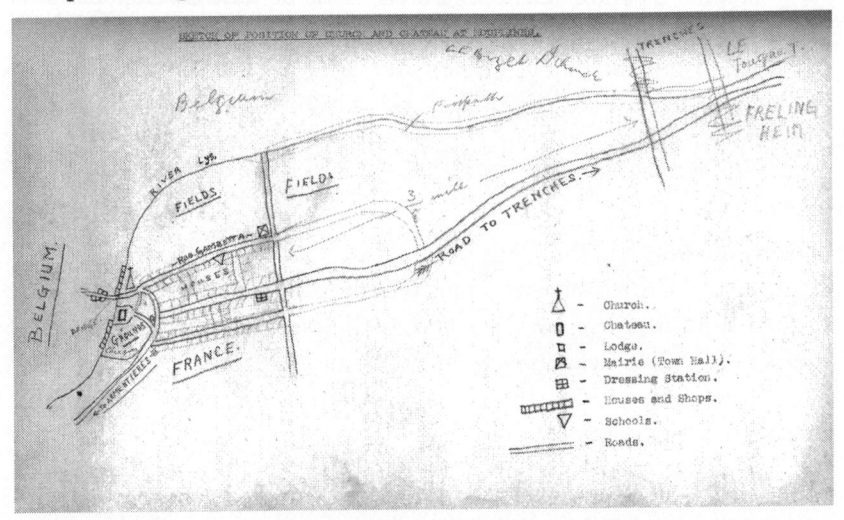

26. Sketch of Position of Church and Chateau at Houplines

Along the road to Houplines a large number of men, women and children were hurrying towards Armentières crying aloud. Upon my asking the reason, I was informed that the Germs were shelling Houplines very heavily, and that a large number of soldiers and civilians had been killed. Many wounded men and horses were afterwards brought along the road.

I was fairly used to shells, and I made up my mind to "carry on", and when I got into Houplines there was no one to be seen - all having cleared out or taken to cellars.

I could see from the smoke of the shells that they were bursting near the Chateau, and I therefore decided to go to the lodge - a distance of some 50 yards from the house - and see if there were any Signallers there who could give me any details of the bombardment.

I had just arrived at the gates when several men came running along the path from the Chateau and told me that everyone except two Signallers - one on duty, and the other as orderly - had been ordered to leave the Chateau, as it was being shelled and also the church just across the road. They also told me that the last shell had burst just outside the room in which the Signallers stayed and that they had all been thrown to the ground by the percussion.

Shells rained in at the Chateau and church for about an hour, and in the meantime we had dinner in the Lodge to prepare ourselves should this be the beginning of an attack.

Our artillery were by no means silent whilst this was going on, but at the end of about two hours the firing suddenly ceased, and everything was still. I then went round the town to see the results, and I will never in all my life forget what I saw.

The church, built in 1575, which, a couple of hours before had been hardly damaged, was now full of shell holes and completely wrecked. Houses and shops were also terribly smashed, and the roads were strewn with wreckage of all descriptions. A bilious yellow - the result of the Lyddite in the shells - was in evidence everywhere and many people who had come in contact with it had yellow skins. Women were running about crying for their husbands and children, and vice versa - for many were buried beneath the ruins.

The sight was indeed ghastly, and an atmosphere of death pervaded the town. Not a dog barked, not a bird sang, for even the animals seemed impressed by the awfulness of the scene.

I learnt that the parish priest, Father Bailleul had been told that the Germs were shelling the church and he went out of his house to go to the church and remove the Blessed Sacrament, when on his way he was hit by a shell and killed instantaneously. This fact added greatly to the general mourning of the town.[28]

The Westminsters suffered many casualties[29] - many of the men killed being personal chums of mine, as the Company to which I belonged suffered the most severely.

---

[28] 1938 See memorial in new church.
[29] flack

France, 12/1/15.

Dear Ma,

I wrote you a couple of days ago & hope you got my letter. It was a rather long.

To-day is very fine although lately there has been much rain, but I am pleased to say that I have not once been caught in the rain. A lot of the country around is under water.

The town I am in is a few miles from a much larger place, & this morning I cycled into this bigger town & saw what I consider as terrible a sight as I have seen out here. It was a beautiful church which the Germans shelled when they were near there. I spoke to some of the townsmen & they told me the following tale:—

On the 6th October last they shelled this church & every day until the 28th of the same month they dropped shells into it until they were driven so far back by the British that it was out of range of their guns. On Sundays especially they dropped most shells in case people went to church there. The church itself presents an awful appearance. The roof is full of holes & the sides also. Of course all the windows were broken. The people have not done any repairing as nearly all the workmen are at the war & except for the fact that the Tabernacle has been removed the church has remained as it stood. As usual two large Crucifixes are intact. One however has much wood broken, but the figure is perfect.

How are Phil & Bob Anscombe? Please let me know.

I want to write a few more letters before going to Benediction, so will close.

Write again tomorrow

Bill

27. Wrecking of a Church

Considering the violence of the bombardment, the Chateau came through the ordeal very well, for although the church was only a few yards away, the Chateau was only hit a few times by smaller shells, and was still habitable.

It was with a very heavy heart that I set out at three o'clock to return to Erquinghem. On my way I met the Catholic Chaplain attached to our division, and received absolution in the street. He had not heard of the death of Father Bailleul, and when I told him he went to Houplines where he took up duties for a time.

In the evening I was on duty from 4.00pm to 8.00pm.

4.5.1915

Tuesday the 4th May, the Germs heavily shelled the Q.W.D. Signal Station in the trenches (known as "Buckingham Palace"), and both the Signallers on duty were killed. It will be remembered that this was the Station where I had spent most of my time in the trenches, and whilst the Westminsters were there the Germs had hardly shelled it. Under the new arrangement the Sherwood Foresters were holding this part of the line, and it is quite possible that if we had been doing so, I might not have been able to write these experiences.

The trenches in front of "Buckingham Palace" on which our men had worked so hard were terribly broken down by shellfire. There is no doubt that the Germs shelled the town and trenches because of the work we had been doing, and they wanted to "put the wind up" us, and put us off attacking.

6.5.1915

I mentioned a page or two back that the Germs had not shelled the Royal Engineers' factory, but about 6.00am on Thursday the 6th May 1915 they dropped three or four shells about 20 yards away from where we were sleeping and caused a fair amount of damage. Although the shells fired from a distance of four to five miles away burst so near, they did not wake me - which shows how one can get used to conditions at the front.

The French employees would not work during the day, as they were afraid the Germs might shell again. I went over the building, which in peacetime was a cotton factory, and had a look at the shell holes and saw the looms, which are used in the process of cotton spinning.

Later in the morning as I was off duty, I walked over the fields into the village of Erquinghem and visited some friends which I had made whilst staying there. On my way back I had a look at the armoured train which had been brought up to do some shooting.

To glance at casually, one would take an armoured train to be an ordinary passenger train, but on inspection the deadly guns show their heads, peeping from the sides and the roof.

In the evening I went into Armentières which when I arrived was being shelled rather heavily. Several buildings were set on fire by incendiary shells and the Military Fire Brigade was ordered to attend to a fire in some schools, which was gaining a rapid hold. As there was a shortage of men on this work I gave a hand to get out the engine and pull it along to the scene of the outbreak, where I also assisted with the hose like a full-blown fireman. As a matter of fact the whole business was rather a joke for it was not proposed to put the fire out, but merely to prevent it spreading, and a Military Fire Brigade is very different from the brigades at home.

A heated argument about the hoses was started by an Irishman giving a hand, which delayed the work somewhat; and by the time we had lit our pipes, tied rags around the holes in the hose, and dodged the shells knocking about, the fire had a good hold. I directed the jet of water where the flames were bursting but I honestly believe that some of the holes in the hose did better work than I.

After an hour or two of this I was thoroughly soaked and as the whole "Brigade" had had enough, we "packed up" and let the fire burn itself out.

I don't mind putting out fires, but when one has to keep one eye on the fire, one on the shells coming over and one on the water emitting from where it should not, it is about time an extra "ration" of eyes be issued.

After this I went to the Cinematograph Theatre which had been opened for the troops.

7.5.1915

On Friday the 7th May, I was due for the trenches so after dinner, as a pontoon boat was going to Houplines I boarded it at one o'clock for my return journey.

At 6.00pm I left for the trenches at Le Touquet (in Belgium) these trenches are on the left bank of the River Lys and to get to them one has to go over the bridge by the church and follow a railway track.

On arriving at the Railway Station one sees a train with the engine attached as if ready to move off, but the number of holes in the carriages would not permit of great comfort for passenger travelling. There is a small Signal Box nearby, and punctually at 7.00am the signalman comes on duty and remains there with his head on his hands until six o'clock in the evening. In a soldiers' expression this Signalman is "ten a penny" - the War having affected his brain - and it will no doubt be a relief when a shell or a bullet puts an appearance in his box - if it has not done so by now.

The Station is about 350 yards behind the trenches, and to get to the front line, one goes into the first house along the road, and a passage, running parallel with the pavement, has been made by knocking big holes in the side walls of the houses. There is also a communication trench nearby in case of trouble.

Two of these houses were still occupied, and are open to the troops as Estaminets, and it is possible to come out of the trenches for a quarter of an hour to get a glass of beer.

In one of these houses two old women and a young girl carry on the business (which needless to say, is very brisk) and it is remarkable how they can stand the strain. There is a curve in the road, which prevents bullets from hitting the house but they continually whiz by, as it is easily within bullet range, and the people dare not go out of their house. The beer is brought to them by Army transport when it is available.

I think I can safely say that in no other part of the line are civilians living so near to the danger zone.

The trenches run through the village, at right angles to the road.

We arrived about 7.30pm, and relieved the Signallers of the Sherwood Foresters, and opened up our Station in the cellar of a house in the fire trench.

8.5.1915

I was on duty from midnight until 8.00am Saturday the 8th May, and after breakfast I walked along the trenches to a spot on the left of the road called the "Post of Honour" - a broken wall in a house 15 yards from the Germs. The next house along the road was in possession of the Bosches.

Now and then greetings are exchanged between the enemies, at other times; bombs, bricks, stones and such like are thrown across causing an unpleasant time for the occupants of the post.

The trenches here are some 100 yards in front of those across the river, and one can get a good side view of the village of Frelingheim and see the damage wrought by our guns and observe the effects of any shelling of the village which might be in progress.

In the evening we received a message relating to the torpedoing of the "Lusitania" and also that Italy might be entering the arena in a few days' time.

9.5.1915

As we were going to blow up a mine early in the morning of Sunday the 9th May at 2.30am we shifted our Station to the Company Officer's dug-out, the cellar in which we were not being considered safe as it was certain the Germs would shell it.

We got our wires fixed and at 4.30am the mine was exploded on our left. The result was a "rise" for some of the Bosches. At the same time artillery and rifle fire commenced and for about an hour we had some "fun". In the evening the Germs played a "dirty trick" on us by shelling the house, the cellar of which we occupied, and worrying us just as we were in the midst of supper. They did so much damage that we had to clear out of the cellar, and build a "buggy" hutch.

10.5.1915

During the afternoon of Monday the 10th May, as the weather was very fine, I went out with another Signaller by the houses' communication trench and through Belgium to Houplines. We took this opportunity of looking at the damage done to the inside of the church by the bombardment a few days ago.

The altar, pulpit and confessionals were smashed; chairs were strewn about; pillars and walls fallen down, but amongst all this ruination the crucifix stood undamaged over the altar and one at the rear of the church was intact as far as the figure was concerned, although the woodwork of the cross was riddled with shrapnel.

11.5.1915

Tuesday the 11th May was very hot and, as things were fairly quiet, I again went out of the trenches to Houplines and had a bathe in the Lys and dinner at "L'Estaminet d'Alice et Suzanne".

13.5.1915

At four o'clock in the morning of Ascension Day, Thursday the 13th May, the Germs blew up a mine. It was not quite under our trench, but a few yards in front, so fortunately our casualties were not very heavy and from a military standpoint would not repay the time taken and the work done.

28. Chateau de la Rose, Houplines after Bombing

14.5.1915

We were relieved by the East Yorks in the evening of Friday the 14th May.

15.5.1915

As the Chateau was not considered the "healthiest" spot in which to be, next day Headquarters were moved to a house in Rue

Gambetta, and the Signallers took possession of an empty house nearby. To celebrate the occasion we had a "house-warming", with dinner at 7.00pm and I acted as cook.

As there were some 20 Signallers and not enough tables, chairs, glasses etc. to go round, we had to make a raid on some of the houses which had been shelled, and help ourselves to the amount of furniture required. The dinner was a great success, and we finished the evening with a "sing-song".

18.5.1915

I cycled to Erquinghem in the morning of Tuesday the 18th May, to relieve the operators for the trenches, and in the evening I went to Battalion Trench Headquarters (in a Chateau a short distance behind the firing line, and very comfortable).

20.5.1915

A division of "Kitchener's Army" arrived in Armentières and one Battalion came into our trenches for 24 hours' experience on Thursday.

22.5.1915

Shelling had been very heavy during the past few days, and as we came out of the trenches during the afternoon of Saturday the 22nd May, we had one or two narrow escapes from "whiz-bangs".

As the Church had been smashed, our pioneers built an altar and decorated a room in a school, which had been shelled opposite the Signallers' abode.

23.5.1915

During breakfast the next day, we saw a number of civilians going into the schools and we wondered at the reason, when somebody mentioned that it was a Sunday. There being a certain amount of doubt about this, I turned up my pocket diary to discover that it was Whit Sunday, 23rd May 1915. I therefore hurried over my duties, and went across the road to the chapel.

In the left-hand corner at the rear, Father Bailleul, who had been killed in the bombardment of his church, was buried, and as this was the first service since then, a sermon relative to the occasion was preached and there were very few people with dry eyes amongst the congregation.

At the end of Mass everyone turned round towards the grave and recited the "De Profundis", and all the other services I attended here finished in this manner.

Later in the morning we had a swim in the river which ran at the bottom of the garden of our house.

24.5.1915

The regiment opposite us in the trenches was the 133rd Saxon, and on Monday the 24th May we received a message as follows:

"Italy has declared War on Austria aaa Addressed all units, repeat if possible 133rd Saxon regiment."

During the night the East Yorks put up a notice board between the lines for the benefit of the Bosches informing them of Italy's entry into the arena.

25.5.1915

In the evening of Tuesday the 25th May we had an excellent concert in the grounds of the school (a room of which had been converted into the chapel), and I attended for a short time only as I was on duty from 9.00pm until midnight.

26.5.1915

Wednesday the 26th May was a glorious day and in the morning we had a swim, and the afternoon saw us struggling along the communication trench, perspiring freely, in our endeavour to reach the firing line and relieve the East Yorks.

We received a rumour that we would in all probability be moving into a "Gas Area" and this was the first indication of the fact that we were about to move to Ypres. We had heard much about gas being used by the Germs and we were by no means overjoyed when we heard officially that we had to leave Houplines for Ypres. On the other hand we had got rather tired of the monotony round our way, and we were rather keen on "having a go" at the Bosches. Our feelings were therefore somewhat mixed, but had we known what we would have to go through, I do not think many men would have been at all keen on shifting.

28.5.1915

After a very hot and tedious day on Friday the 28th May we were relieved in the trenches by the Cambridgeshire Regiment at about 7.00pm. They had come from Hill 60, and they told us tales of gas and fighting there to cheer us up.

We got into Houplines at about 7.30pm, and started round to say "goodbye" to Suzanne et Alice, Antoinette, the cake-shop girl, and the other friends of the Signal Section. Tears were plentiful for the inhabitants were sorry to lose us, and we on the other hand were sorry to leave before attacking Frelingheim.

At 10.30pm we massed in a field in front of the 43rd Battery, and at 11.00pm moved off. The Germs seemed to have some knowledge of our movements and "got the wind up", firing very heavily into the field just as we had left, and fortunately there were no casualties.

We passed through Armentières, where we had our first rest. All was still, and no one was to be seen. The roar of gunnery and rifle fire could be heard, intermixed with the steady thud of the marching of the Battalion. We were gradually getting further away from the firing line than we had been for six months.

I might here mention that many of our bicycles had "been put out of action" during the past few months, and therefore as there were not enough to go round, some of the Signallers had to march instead of cycle. I volunteered to do the march on the first day, and on the second day I cycled.

We crossed Pont Nieppe, passed through the village of Nieppe and at 4.30am just as the light appeared, reached Bailleul after passing the Aviation Station and various A.S.C. (Army Service Corps) depots, where there was a lot of work being done, for night time is when most work is done as regards rations.

We "put up" at an empty house for the "night". We had marched some 12 miles, which considering the fact that we had been in the trenches without exercise for a number of months and had come straight out of them, was no small matter, especially with full pack, rifle and equipment, and by the time we reached our billet, we were for the most part, absolutely "done".

29.5.1915

We "got up" at 9.00am and I was on cycling duty for the orderly room all morning. At 2.00pm we paraded and marched to a field a mile or so away where we were inspected by Sir John French, who made an appropriate speech, during which time an aeroplane started from an adjacent field for the firing line, making a considerable amount of noise and preventing us from hearing the latter portion of his oration.

In the afternoon I continued on duty as Battalion Cyclist, finishing at 8.00pm, by which time I was fairly exhausted, the roads being hilly and cycling tiring, especially after the march of the evening before. I got my things together preparatory to moving off tomorrow, and "turned in" on the floor for a night's sleep undisturbed by shellfire - the first for over six months.

30.5.1915

We arose at 3.45am on Sunday the 30th May, and the Brigade paraded and moved off at 5.00am; the Queen's Westminsters leading the Brigade; the Signallers leading the Battalion; and I leading the Signallers.

It was fairly warm, and although I cycled, it was a very tiring journey as we were all feeling the effects of the past two days.

We passed through the borders of France and Belgium, as the people of the village were going to church, and reached Poperinghe at 9.00am - a distance of 15 miles.

We were allotted to fields about a mile from Poperinghe in which to spend our time, and we began making things as comfortable as possible for our night's rest.

We were not allowed into Poperinghe, but with the aid of an official envelope and my cycle, I managed to get out and have a look round the town.

Poperinghe is a fair sized town, and one is at once struck with the atmosphere of cleanliness - very different from Armentières. At this time it had not suffered very severely from shellfire, but the church had several gaping holes in its roof and sides.

In the evening we had a "sing-song" in the field, and as night began to fall we lit fires, and continued our impromptu concert.

We were about to "turn in" when it commenced to rain, so under cover of darkness, I stole into the next field where there was a partially cut hay-rick, and took up my quarters there for the night. It was very comfortable, and much better than the open ground, and I would be pleased to recommend this form of bed in the event of one not having the real thing.

There was a terrific bombardment during the night, and we all thought that there was a big battle raging around Ypres, but we afterwards discovered to our cost that it was quite usual for the district, and this evening was by no means out of the ordinary.

29. Cloth Hall 1913

31.5.1915

We "arose" at 7.30am on Monday the 31st May, and after a wash in a very dirty pond felt much refreshed, even though somewhat wet, for our "Bivvy".

I went for a cycle ride during the morning across the border into France to a village by name Abelle where I purchased some "grub" for dinner. During the afternoon we made our preparations for moving up to the trenches.

At 6.30pm with "D" Company, I boarded a motor bus marked "Shepherd's Bush", which took us to the outskirts of Vlamertinghe. On our way we spotted a Zeppelin very high in the air, and this was the first I had seen.

Along the road on either side were marvellously strong defences in case of our having to fall back, ammunition columns, batteries of artillery, resting places for men back from the trenches, and the whole route was lined with khaki life, and men full of cheerfulness.

The name of Ypres to us who so far had not seen any severe fighting, was enough to make us quiet and thoughtful and as an indication of my personal feelings I wrote in my pocket diary whilst travelling in the motor bus - "Motor bus to Ypres" - so that in the event of my terminating my earthly existence the destination I was making for would be known.

I am not a sentimentalist but neither my, nor any other man's pen, could describe what we saw and felt during the next few hours sufficiently to indicate or convey the sights, or our feelings to another with any degree of reality. I will however in simple language do my utmost.

We marched through Vlamertinghe as the day was drawing to a close, and no longer did we see men stationary, but along the road we discerned through the darkness men returning from the trenches, either relieved from the firing line, or having been taking up rations, ammunition, stores, or any other of the numerous requirements.

Indian troops marching with unearthly quietness, Scotch and Irishmen with a strong brogue saying cheerfully: "Good luck, boys" and other expressions - their spirits being high on being relieved from the trenches, having come through safely in such a terrible portion of the line.

It was a pitch black night and we were still a mile away from Ypres, when we halted for a rest in a field on the side of the road, where we got our final directions about going through Ypres, the chief being that we were to "double" over a bridge across the moat[30] at which the Germs continually fired and had the range; and that we would not get another rest until we reached the trenches.

We were sitting on the ground when all of a sudden there was a brilliant flash and a tremendous explosion about 50 yards to our rear. It was one of our big guns firing from a short distance behind us, but at the time we could not tell whether it was our guns or a bursting shell. Our nerves were very highly strung and in a soldiers' expression "that did it".

At 10.00pm we "fell in" and on our way marched up a slight hill and from the top saw Ypres in flames in four or five places.

---

[30] Menin Gate.

We went down the other side of the hill and entered the outskirts of the town, and experienced more shells during the next few hours than we had seen in all our time on active service.

We past the picturesque water tower on the left, which was the only object nearby which had not been hit, the asylum and the jail almost in ruins, and saw at the end of the road the tower of the Cathedral looming in the light of a house on fire just opposite, the sparks of which fell on us as we marched past. We turned to the right and saw the remnants of the houses - once such fine buildings but now a mass of ruins - and on our left the Cloth Hall, which at that time had a couple of pillars standing at either end, although all the higher portions of the centre were gone.

Such a scene of desolation as I shall never forget met my gaze. The beautiful Cathedral, the grand old Cloth Hall, the mansions, business houses, all treated in the same manner, and yet the Germs did not seem content, for all the time shells were screaming over our heads and falling into portions of the town.

Great holes were in the roadway and masses of masonry had fallen across our path and as we came to them, we passed the "word" back: "mind the shell-hole" or "mind the bricks", all in a whisper for although we were still a mile away from the Bosches, the awfulness of the scene so impressed us.

We turned to the left in front of the Cloth Hall into the wide market square and then into a narrow road which was completely in ruins leading to the bridge across the moat over which we ran in small parties, not only "as if our lives depended upon it" but actually our lives did depend upon our getting across the bridge quickly.

The cemetery was on our left, and had been shelled terribly, and the smell was very obnoxious. Ypres itself smelt vilely on account of the number of people buried beneath the ruins, but it is as a bottle of scent compared with a strong cheese or a bad egg when the cemetery is concerned.

We were now in open country and it was a treat to get a breath of fresh air.

We got down the hill by Potiejze Wood along which smashed houses were dotted at intervals, for the Germs had done their deadly work with great thoroughness worthy of a better cause, and in the district of Ypres and the salient there is not a house even slightly damaged - all as far as possible razed to the ground.

We reached the third line of trenches at 11.30pm and got "sorted out" by midnight, when I went on duty on the wire for a couple of hours, after which, in spite of the terrible noise of the shelling, I fell into a deep slumber.

These details read in the daylight do not perhaps cause great emotions, but the night on which we made our first entry into Ypres was one of the worst I have ever known. I have since been through the town of Ypres many times, cycling and marching, and except when there was a battle raging in the vicinity, the shelling has not been so severe as on this night, and the town is not always on fire. Added to this was the darkness and our nerves, which left much to be desired, and one's feelings on seeing such solitude (for of course there is nobody living near) are very sentimental, and the fires with no one attempting to arrest their progress, caused a sensation as never before experienced.

I have several pictures of the destruction of Ypres but they are not for me - I do not want anything to remind me of the ruins of Ypres - for the sights witnessed on this evening will be with me to my dying day as vividly as they appeared on the night on which I made my first entry into the town of YPRES.

30. Cloth Hall after Bombing

31. Short Street of Ypres after Bombing

32. In the Heart of Ypres after Bombing

CHAPTER 4

Belgium

From 1st June 1915 until 9th August 1915

1.6.1915

It was indeed difficult to keep awake during my tour of duty from midnight until 2.00am on Tuesday the 1st June 1915 and I was very thankful when it was time for me to sleep.

I was again on duty from 8.00am until 10.00am, during which time I partook of a biscuit and some "Bully". After this I once more "turned in" until duty again called and then we all had a meal (4.00pm) which, however, resembled very closely the previous one, as no fires were allowed to be lit on account of the smoke caused, which would inform the Bosches that these trenches were occupied and so call forth a shower of shells.

There are a great number of lines of trenches in this district, many of which are not occupied, and it is interesting to watch the Germs shelling empty trenches - they no doubt thinking that the casualties inflicted were very heavy - and putting it in their "official communiqué".

All day the bombardment on every side was absolutely awful and we all had severe headaches but of course had to "stick it".

2.6.1915

On Wednesday the 2nd June we watched the Germs have another "go" at the tower of the Cathedral, and they struck it several times scattering chunks of masonry in all directions.

In the evening we moved along about half-a-mile to our right; the right flank of the Battalion holding the railway line by the Menin Road.

Until this time our regiment had the long-pattern rifle and a short bayonet, whilst the rest of the Brigade had the short rifle and long sword.

The short rifle weighs about one pound less than the long, and it is more convenient and easier to manipulate, so that as the men got killed or wounded in the other Battalions of our Brigade, we had their rifles and swords. There were also a large number of arms and equipment of men who had been killed in a recent attack lying in front of our line in the open, and at night we would steal out and hunt for them, and share out.

3.6.1915

I got my fresh rifle and sword on Thursday the 3rd June and it was very clean and had an excellent barrel.

4.6.1915

On Friday the 4th June the Germs shelled us on three different occasions; the first two times doing very little damage but during the third shelling, one percussion shell fell right in the trench amongst the men of my Company and this one shell killed nine of my chums, wounded seven others, and three sustained shell-shock.

I would here like to mention the names of three killed, who were particularly my "pals", they were:

> Corporal Matthews
> Rifleman Kerl, and
> Rifleman Mac. Gillervray
> R.I.P.

The Stretcher Bearers went immediately to their aid, and one of them whilst carrying out his duties was himself severely wounded by another shell.

The shell, which killed so many of these fine fellows, went through the parapet and the men were buried under the debris. They were dug out but were found to be beyond recognition. The names of the killed were discovered by calling the roll. This terrible result was the work of one single shell. Several other shells, to the extent of about 50, were fired at us, causing a number of other casualties, more or less severe.

During the night a burial party made a large hole just behind the trenches in which to bury their remains, and whilst on this unpleasant task came across a number of other bodies, and as the morning light was about to appear, our men had to be buried in the same spot.

5.6.1915

We were again shelled very heavily on Saturday the 5th June and the West Yorks had a large number of casualties. Our ration party was caught by a machine gun, and several men received leg wounds, which provided for them a "ticket to Blighty".

I doubt if there was a day passed without a number of casualties whilst the Battalion was in the trenches in the salient so I will not refer to the casualties except on special occasions, otherwise this will prove too sad and monotonous reading.

In the evening "A" and "B" companies moved up into the fire trench. On account of gas; the danger of working in the daylight; and other reasons work on the trenches was always done during the night, and no man slept between the hours of sunset and sunrise, but during the day.

6.6.1915

We had just "turned in" at 6.00am on Sunday the 6th June, when the Germs commenced a heavy bombardment on our trench, which continued until about 9.00am, so we lost three hours' sleep on this day. We were, however getting used to this continued shelling and were now able to sleep through quite a heavy cannonade, so long as the shells did not come too near. The weather was very hot, and we had one of our men down with sunstroke.

7.6.1915

Nothing very special took place on Monday the 7th June but as usual we had a number of casualties, and there was plenty of 'tillery "knocking about".

8.6.1915

After a very sultry and "noisy" day (guns and thunder), on Tuesday the 8th June, we were relieved from the trenches at 11.00pm, and as we were going out the Germs treated us to a "dose" of shrapnel, and Lance-Corporal Newcombe of the Signal Section was wounded for a second time.

If anyone wants to have a little excitement, I would suggest, in the dark, running up the hill from Potiejze Wood on a hot night, with full pack, rifle, equipment and 250 rounds of ammunition, and at the same time "dodge" shells by means of "belly-flopping" (throwing one's self down in the roadway or ditch).

9.6.1915

We marched through Ypres without any further excitement as the Bosches were not shelling the town, and got on our way to some huts between Ypres and Vlamertinghe where we were to stay, and at which we arrived at 2.30am on Wednesday the 9th June. We were served out with some hot tea, after which we "turned in" and "turned out" again at 9.00am.

There was a great shortage of water in this district and we were not allowed to wash with fresh water, so as to save it. There was however a stagnant pool a short distance away, so we made our ablutions there, although this was also forbidden on account of its filthy state.

Whilst coming out of the trenches last night, one of the Signallers "belly-flopped" and lost his telegraphic instrument, and as an excuse to look round Ypres in the daylight, I offered to go with him, and try and find it. (One man is not allowed to go by himself in case he is hit, and wants aid.)

We therefore obtained the necessary permission, with directions that we were to cycle through the town as quickly as possible, and we started off on our bicycles at about 2.30pm.

Having got somewhat used to the conditions of affairs in Ypres, we were not so staggered by the sights, but rather looked on them in the light of sightseers - especially as it was daylight.

I must admit that we got off our "bikes" and walked slowly through, and by this means had a good opportunity of looking thoroughly at the town. On the sides of the road the bones and skeletons of dead animals, which had been burnt (as the best and healthiest means of their disposal), were stacked in small piles, many of which were still burning.

We walked round the Cathedral and Cloth Hall but as the day was hot and the smell correspondingly strong, to say nothing of a few shells coming unpleasantly near, we did not stay long in this vicinity but made our way to the easterly portion of the town by the moat. As however, the cemetery was nearby it was not too nice to be at this spot either. We had a look at the graves, many of which had gaping holes in them, and the tomb stones smashed to atoms.

Without having found the instrument, we "about turned" and again went through Ypres, and got on the road to Vlamertinghe (about two miles behind) and made a few purchases, returning to our "rest" camp at six o'clock.

I created somewhat of a record at letter writing during the evening. I went on duty at 10.30pm and wrote letters without a break until four o'clock on Thursday, the 10th June, when I came off duty and slept until 8am.

10.6.1915

It being considered that we had had a good "rest" (nearly two days) we moved up to a line of trenches on the banks of the Yser canal.

The actual trenches were about 20 yards from the river, but as they were about a mile from the front line, we did not stay in them, but in "dug-outs" built in the banks, which sloped steeply towards the river.

This position was considered very nice as there was a tow-path along which one could walk, and bathing was also permitted, and the Germs did not shell this spot more than two or three times daily.

(After a time, however, bathing had to be stopped on account of the Bosches dropping their dead into the river, which flowed in our direction. Later on a Germ shell broke the lock gates and the water ran out, leaving only a small depth, the greater part of which was mud.)

As there were not enough "buggy-hutches" to go round, the Signallers set to work to build one. We dug out a deep square in the banks, about 9ft by 6ft and completed this operation by 9.00pm. It was too dark to finish this evening, so we arranged some poles across the top, and put our waterproof above, and were just about to settle down for the night when it began to rain, and it ended in a deluge continuing through the night. Of course the rain broke down our temporary roof, and we got the full benefit of the water, but never daunted, we lay down and covered ourselves with some sacking.

Although I had had only four hours' rest the previous evening, I could not get to sleep as the rain made so much noise, and kept beating against my face. The others being in the same predicament, we decided to stand up for a time, until the rain stopped, in a corner which had a space where the rain could not gain admittance.

We chatted for about four hours, and were all thoroughly soaked, when we heard a call for "Stretcher Bearers". We went out, and discovered that the rain had caused a "dug-out" to collapse, and bury four men. We therefore set to work to remove the earth and take them out, and managed to save three, the fourth however being beyond aid by the time we got at him.

This, none too pleasant occupation, made us nice and warm and with the aid of the wood from the broken "buggy" we made a good roof for ours, which kept the rain out and after a cup of tea (made with fairly warm water boiled on candle ends) we "turned in" at 5.30am for the night.

12.6.1915

As dusk was falling on Saturday, the 12th June, a Zeppelin flew over our trenches at a quite low altitude. The night was very dark and the "Zepp" was spotted quite accidentally by a man walking along the trench. We immediately reported the event (I was on duty), and were afterwards informed that the message reached London in 12 minutes.

During the afternoon the Germs shelled heavily the village of Vlamertinghe.

13.6.1915

On Sunday morning I was rather anxious to get to church if possible, and as a cyclist was wanted to go with a dispatch to the Transport Lines (between Vlamertinghe and Poperinghe) I made arrangements, and got permission to go to Mass in the church at Vlamertinghe.

I started off at 8.00am and skirted Ypres, and arrived at Vlamertinghe in about half an hour.

The church was the object of the Germs' shelling the previous day, and it had been set on fire by incendiary shells, and now only the walls were standing, and it was still burning. It had indeed been a stately church, and the tall tower, although it had been hit, was still standing. The Germs' desire, no doubt, was to smash the tower, but in this they were frustrated, as I was from attending Mass.

Apart from the Church, the village itself had not been severely damaged, and people were still living nearby. (I have lately met men from this district and am told that Vlamertinghe is now a mass of ruins, and Poperinghe is almost as bad).

I got to the transport, and returned to the trenches after delivering my message and had a swim in the river.

14.6.1915

During the evening of Monday the 14th June, we went into the environs of Ypres "finding" tables, chairs, and other furniture for our "dug-out".

15.6.1915

On Tuesday the 15th June we were told to be in readiness for an attack which we were to make on a line of the German trenches near Hooge and as this was our first attack we were rather excited, and we had a swim to cool down. We were to be in the second line, and half of the Battalion was to move into the trench as soon as the line was taken.

The Battalion moved up at 8.30pm, but as I was detailed to wait until relieved by a Brigade Signaller, I went forward at 10.30pm with the Colonel and Adjutant.

It was a terribly dark night, and we made our way over a number of fields containing many shell holes, and we occasionally came to earth. The Germ's star shells however, helped us considerably to see our way, and after traversing about three miles of fields we arrived on the left of the village of Hooge at midnight.

With another Signaller, I had to open a new Station about a hundred yards away from Headquarters in case the Battalion got cut off, so that as soon as I arrived I had to lay a wire and get connected up. This work was completed in about half an hour, and it consisted of a great deal of travelling on the stomach as the Germs were firing rather heavily, and the line was laid above the trenches. After completing we managed each to get an hour's sleep before operations commenced.

16.6.1915

At 2.30am on Wednesday the 16th June, our artillery sent out "feelers" and at 2.45am the bombardment commenced in deadly earnest. The daylight had hardly appeared, but the bursting of the shells lit up very vividly the lines of trenches. The Germs replied at once by shelling our trenches with high explosives of a heavy calibre and the noise of the guns and the bursting shells was terrific.

Within an hour, three times our telephone line was broken, and I had to go out over the top and mend it. Unfortunately there was a farm in front of our line and the Germs shelled it heavily in case ammunition was stored there. Our wires ran at the side of the farm, and consequently were so often broken. After a bombardment of an hour and a half, the front line charged and as we were told later, altogether four lines of trenches were taken on a front of about a thousand yards.

For four hours this ceaseless bombardment continued, and at 6.40am we received the following message:

"All goes well aaa We have captured the enemy's first line."

Just before receiving this message we were wondering how things were progressing in front, and were rather worried about having no news, when we saw a batch of Germ prisoners under our guard coming along the Menin Road. This informed us that we had at least been successful in breaking through.

For some reason or other the Germs fired on their prisoners coming along the road and the prisoners and our guard had to scatter and lie down for a time, but none tried to escape, but hurried to a place of safety where they paraded together and marched off under the guard.

It is possible that the Germs fired on their own men on the principle that "dead men tell no tales" but whether this be the case or not, they did it intentionally for they could distinguish the Germs from the British and could have held their fire from the spot where they were.

The bombardment continued fiercely until about 1.00pm and on our men reaching the second line, the Germs counter-attacked with great severity, but were repulsed, and our casualties mounted high.

We received the following message about midday:

"The Third Division reports situation rather obscure aaa After reaching the enemy's second line of trenches on a line running from a point J.13A 4.5 in a S.S.E. direction through BELLEWAAR FARM to about J.12D 1.2 the Germs shelled very heavily and our line had to retire in places aaa The Germs commenced a counter-attack against centre of line aaa This counter-attack appears to have been driven back by the observation of the F.O.O. (Forward Observation Officer) who could see enemy retiring and losing heavily from our rifle and gunfire aaa About 100 prisoners belonging to 27 reserve division and 15th Corps have been taken."

The approximate times of taking the trenches were:

First line	-	4.15am
Second line	-	6.00am
Third line	-	8.15am
Fourth line	-	later in the morning

Only a small party penetrated the fourth line and they had to retire as the Germs counter-attacked before more men could be got up. For safety's sake our men also retired from the third line as the trenches were so badly smashed that they afforded practically no protection.

During the afternoon the Germs sent over a few gas shells, but the wind being rather strong it was very little use to them, and we did not even put on our respirators.

The afternoon was somewhat quieter, but the battle commenced again at six o'clock when the Germs subjected us to a very severe bombardment for an hour, which they followed up with a strong attack, and our men had to retire. We now held only one line.

For some purpose - the reason of which I cannot say - during this counter-attack our guns were practically silent.[31]

The Germs were bombarding us terribly and our men were falling over like ninepins, but not one of our guns as far as we could tell, belched forth their death-dealing missiles until the Germs were about to attack when they opened up with shrapnel practically making a curtain of fire. This procedure may be the best if the Signalling wires are not broken and the S.O.S. message (the call sent when the enemy is seen to leave the trench to attack) can be got through to the batteries' artillery, but if the lines are broken, which invariably is the case, it has to be left to the infantry to repel the attack after they have been subjected to a severe bombardment.

---

[31] ? Shortage of shells

I do not think that at this time it was a case of shortage of shells[32] for we saw tremendous stocks of ammunition in certain places before the attack and some artillerymen to whom we were speaking said that it had been brought up for our attack and that we had more handy.

The same procedure was carried out at Hooge on the 9th August (about which more later) when the papers said that it was the first engagement when we could say that we had enough shells, and it seems to me that it has rather a demoralising effect and I should certainly say that all our men would have felt happier, if only a few of our guns had been firing on the Germs' trenches.

As evening fell the firing became more normal and the night passed without any further attack, we holding one line on a ridge on the left of the village of Hooge.

Twice during the night the Germs broke our wire, and I had to go out and mend it, but although it is more difficult to trace the break, it is not such a bad job as when it had to be mended in daylight under observation of the Bosches.

The importance of keeping up communications cannot be exaggerated, for if the line is broken messages have to be taken by hand and apart from the length of time this method takes, it is very dangerous for the Signaller, who may not get through.

17.6.1915

The Germs did not counter-attack on Thursday the 17th June the reason no doubt being that the night had given us an opportunity of consolidating our gain. During the morning the Germs happened to "fire" one of our ammunition stores, and a great deal of noise resulted thereby, the heat making the bullets explode, but apart from the waste, no damage was done.

There being no signs of another counter-attack by mid-day, I decided to "turn in" (for we had been up all the night) when the Germs broke our wire, and again I had to mend it.

---

[32] ?

The regiments taking part in this attack besides our own were:

> Liverpool Scottish (the regiment which came over in the boat with us to France),
> Royal Scots, and
> Northumberland Fusiliers.

I understand that the Liverpool Scottish who made an attack immediately on our right lost about 50% of their men. The official report for such an engagement would be:

"Some ground was gained around the Ypres Salient on the 16th instant".

I was informed that about 50 Germs dropped their rifles and surrendered to the Royal Scots, but I cannot vouch for this statement, although there is no reason why it should not be true.

At 10.00pm we were relieved and went to the line of trenches on the canal bank where we rested for the night.

18.6.1915

We did not rise until a late hour on Friday the 18th June, and after a swim in the river, we had a good breakfast (tea, ham and bread).

During the afternoon I went with an officer to arrange billets for the Battalion in which to rest, in huts between Vlamertinghe and Poperinghe. The huts between Ypres and Vlamertinghe at which we had stayed previously had been shelled and were untenable. At 10.30pm I met the Battalion on the main road and guided them in, and myself "turned in" about midnight.

19.6.1915

A walk through the woods in the morning, and a cycle ride into Poperinghe to obtain tinned pineapple (Crosse and Blackwell's) in the afternoon, was my programme for Saturday the 19th June 1915.

It was about this time that it became possible to obtain luxuries unheard of at the Front before, such as tinned fruit, condensed milk and other commodities (at a price) similar to those obtained at home, and they were indeed a God-send. As an indication of the price, however a fair sized tin of fruit cost 2.50 francs (about two shillings), and riches were indeed a blessing in these circumstances.

20.6.1915

On Sunday morning, the 20th June, I attended Mass which was held in a field nearby, with Signaller T. Buckley (since killed in action, R.I.P.) and in the afternoon had a sleep in the woods.

I was on duty from 4.00pm until 8.00pm and an interesting message was sent showing our strength. The strength of an infantry Battalion is about 1,000, and our strength after the attack was:

Riflemen	370
Signallers, machine gunners, stretcher bearers, etc.	120
Sergeants, corporals and transport	203

	693

which shows a deficit of 300 men.

21.6.1915

During the evening of Monday the 21st June, an open-air concert to which we invited the East Yorkshire Regiment, was held and much appreciated.

22.6.1915

I walked to Vlamertinghe for a "bath" at 6.30am on Tuesday the 22nd June 1915, and was on duty for the rest of the day as the Battalion Cyclist.

23.6.1915 and 24.6.1915

Wednesday and Thursday were days of practically complete rest and preparation for another turn in the trenches.

25.6.1915

The weather had been very good the past few days and on Friday, the 25th June we were for the trenches again and we decided that the dryness would permit of our going by a roadway called "High Street", made by the engineers through fields, and so avoid going along the main road which was subject to heavy shellfire.

When the weather was dry "High Street" was quite good, and as a matter of fact, easier to march on than the cobbled road running through Ypres.

At 1.30pm we left the huts, taking a hand cart (obtained in Ypres) in which to put our Signalling stores, and reckoned to do the distance of about eight miles to the trenches by about four o'clock.

We had pushed our cart for about two miles singing cheerily, when the "clerk of the weather" decided that the rain was wanted for the crops, and we got caught in a severe thunderstorm. Our ardour was severely damped, and the cart began to pick up a large portions of the fields (to which it was not entitled) and expected us to push it along with its ill-gotten gains adhering to its wheels. (It must have seen some of us in Ypres.)

I cannot say the number of times it got stuck, but the language occasioned by this cart must really have made it feel ashamed to have been built. I will say however, that when on a hot day one has a thick uniform, equipment, pack, rifle and ammunition; and an uncomfortable waterproof sheet over one's shoulders, which persists in placing the rain in one spot to soak through the clothes, it is no joke to push a cart laden with heavy instruments, which does not agree to be pushed. Another point which makes things awkward is the number of shell holes which have to be negotiated. Twice when the size of the shell hole did not permit of its being skirted, we rushed it down the hole, and up the other side, and sad to relate, twice did the cart overturn, depositing its goods in the mud and losing various portions of itself.

We tried to hurry on as the Signallers in the trenches were waiting to be relieved, but after a time we had to abandon the idea of hurrying and took it gently. The rain lessened slightly, and we got to a cobbled road on the North of Ypres where we sat down for a rest, thinking we had finished with "High Street".

The climax was reached when we were all lying down on the wet ground somewhat exhausted, when a colonel came along and we did not get up and salute. The colonel stopped and called the sergeant and demanded why we had not stood up and saluted! The sergeant explained that "in the field" it is not necessarily to salute, but the colonel said it was, and reprimanded the sergeant adding: "I suppose you have just come out here, and think you can do as you like". On being informed that we had already been eight months overseas (which was probably much more than he) he seemed surprised, but said we were to remember another time. We were all standing by this time as we had been spoken to, and as he left we gave him a "salute", and I think it as well that he did not see it - nice man.

By this time the rain had increased, and we went a long distance out of our way to avoid "High Street", and got to the canal bank by 6.30pm. There being no chance of tea, we crossed the pontoon bridge, and on inquiring our way to the particular trenches we wanted, we were informed, unfortunately, that we had to continue along "High Street".

Two of the Signallers were so exhausted that we left them on the canal bank to rest in the rain, while we pushed on to the village of La Brique for which we were making. The rain was still coming down in torrents, and the last stage of the journey across small fields was indeed the "limit", and by this time, we were soaked to the skin.

We got to La Brique at seven o'clock and by the side of a house, full of shell holes, an officer of the Leinster Regiment was standing, and upon seeing us covered in mud, smiled broadly, and asked us if we were having a nice time. On our assuring him to the contrary, he told us to "come in" (through a shell hole in the side) and he gave us all a cup of hot tea and some biscuits; which proves that all officers are not typical of the colonel referred to in a previous page.

We put our cart in the garden of a house nearby, which was being used as a Dressing Station (First Aid Post). The garden was really a cemetery for it contained a large number of graves of British soldiers who had been killed near the spot, and I may mention that before we came out of the trenches here, we had added quite a large number of the Queen's Westminsters to this burial ground.

The rain ceased soon after we arrived here, and we waited until it was fairly dark so as to walk above ground and "risk it" rather than take the communication trench, which we knew would be full of water, and we arrived and relieved the Leinster Signallers at 9.30pm; only about two or three hours late.

The trenches were full of water, but that did not matter for we were already as wet as we could be. The rain, however, did us a good "turn" for it had ruined the line to Headquarters, and they had been running their messages by hand and to open the Station it would be necessary to lay a fresh wire. There was another Signaller with me and we were both so "fed up" and miserable that we decided to say nothing about there being no line, and of course Headquarters could not communicate with us and tell us to lay one, so we "turned in" after waiting up until midnight when the rest of the Battalion came in, and we put them in their sectors according to companies. There was a great shortage of "dug-outs" and many men had to sleep out in the open trench.

26.6.1915

We were heavily shelled at 5.30am and 6.30am on Saturday the 26th June but, except for four casualties, nothing out of the ordinary took place.

27.6.1915

It was decided to lay our line during the evening, but as the supply of wire was not forthcoming, we had to leave it for a time. We were quite willing, and "turned in" at 9.30pm and did not wake until 7.00am the next morning, when we were shouted at to get out of our "dug-out" as a shell had gone clean through the next but one to us.

We, however, felt as safe in our little "buggy" as out, and stayed there until the shelling had ceased, and then had another couple of hours' sleep. Sleeping during the night is forbidden around Ypres, but one gets into no trouble if not found out. Arrangements for work are made during the night and for sleep during the day.

It was decided that no Station was necessary where we were, as there was another about a hundred yards along the trench, so we returned to Headquarters, and I acted as cook for the Signallers there. During the night we built a "spanking" "dug-out".

My duties as cook did not take up a great deal of time, the chief work connected with it being a walk out of the trenches every evening to the village of La Brique, for the rations.

28.6.1915 and 29.6.1915

I made my journeys for rations during the nights of Monday and Tuesday, and the Germs gave our "dumping" ground at La Brique a good number of shells, and also gave our trenches more than were required to allow us to have a comfortable time.

30.6.1915

As a punishment our artillery around Ypres received orders to shell heavily the Germs' trenches, objects behind and also any of the enemies' transport and "dumping" ground, on Wednesday the 30th June, for one hour, commencing at 8.45pm. We were told officially that there would be an "artillery display" at this time to celebrate the half year, so I got to La Brique early and went into a house which had been shelled and climbed to the roof, and with my tried friend, my pipe - without which I could never have existed in the trenches - I watched through a shell hole as beautiful and terrible a sight imaginable.

The shell bursts kept lighting up the little village, throwing out the ruins in relief, and all round for miles one could see only a mass of fire.

The Germs did not reply. It seems as if they were "flabbergasted" by the magnitude of the display, and were waiting to see at which part of the line an attack was contemplated, if one was coming.

For an hour the sky was continually alight with bursting shells, making the blood red sunset more intense as it slowly passed away. Big shells, small shells, screeching above one's head, and bursting without a break with tremendous force. If for a second or two no shell burst, the noise seemed more intense as a contrast, and it sounded as if hell had been let loose.

All the roar of the guns ceased as suddenly as it had commenced, and the crack of rifles and machine guns could be heard, and this gradually died down; but for two hours I had to wait before it was safe to risk going down the road to the trenches. It would have meant certain death to have gone before.

No doubt the Germs were surprised at nothing happening, but we wait our time, and this was only an indication of what we could do. Six months of the year is completed, and we still wait, for we are not ready to strike, but the time is coming......

1.7.1915

It was a very fine day on Thursday the 1st July, and I did my duty as cook.

We were very heavily shelled all day, and in the evening when I journeyed to La Brique things were very lively, and a continuous bombardment was kept up along the road which I was going, so I decided that the pleasanter way would be across fields in the rear.

2.7.1915

On Friday the 2nd July I carried out my usual duties as cook. During the day the Germs fired some shells round our way, and one fell just behind our trench, but did not explode. As it was dangerous to men walking up to the fire trench, it was decided to explode it when there were no men about; so, after smothering it with sand bags, a fuse was attached and it was fired.

It exploded satisfactorily and no damage was done. A minute or two afterwards a strong odour of flowers, such as one might smell in a death chamber, was evident, and we then discovered that it was an asphyxiating shell we had exploded, and we had "gassed" ourselves. A rush was therefore made for gas helmets, and although for a time it made our eyes "smart", no one was seriously affected.

3.7.1915

During the night of Saturday the 3rd July, we were relieved from the fire trench, and went into the second line. Our new quarters were about eight hundred yards from the Bosches and the line of trenches ran behind a thick hedge, completely obscuring the Germs' view, but we could see through loopholes.

Behind the hedge a round tub had been placed, and from a ditch nearby I filled the tub, and proceeded to have a bath.

I got on very nicely and was about to dry myself, when the Germs sent over a "salvo" of shrapnel and I had to run for cover. Evidently they had noticed my "white" skin between some gaps in the hedge and they objected to my ablutions without their authority.

During the afternoon the Germs bombarded us very severely and also sent over to us our first serious supply of gas and gas shells. We donned our respirators, and saw that our rifles were in trim with a nice sharp bayonet attached thereto, and awaited developments. No attack came, however, and after a couple of hours we took off our respirators, but the gas hung about for many hours afterwards, and the smell gave all of us a sickly feeling.

The noise of a large gas shell going through the air is very peculiar, sounding like a tube train when one is waiting at an underground station, but when the shell arrives, unfortunately it does not stop at any particular spot as does a train, but bursts where one does not want it to, with a loud bang, sending out clouds of smoke and gas.

A matter of about a hundred yards away from the line of trenches in which we were, was the village of St Jean, which was practically ruined. The church and cemetery around had been shelled, but the church tower was still standing.

At 7.00pm the Germs started a systematic shelling of this tower, and from my little "dug-out" I watched them trying to bring this tower to the ground. Their shooting was really splendid; but even though they fired about 50 shells, they had to give it up, for the tower had very thick walls, and was most substantially built.

The cemetery attached was quite small yet every shell fired either hit the tower or church, or else fell among the graves, and as the Bosches were firing from a distance of four to five miles (estimated by the time between hearing the report of the gun and the bursting of the shell) this performance was quite good.

Unfortunately the wind was blowing in the direction from the church to our trenches, and the smell was really terrible, and actually necessitated our wearing gas helmets. Apart from this, however, it was a very interesting sight to watch from so near a point of vantage, and it gave us an opportunity of betting on whether the "next" shell would hit the tower, or fall in our own trenches. (3 to 1 was the limit obtainable.)

The Brigade telegraph wires ran through this village of St Jean, and the shells had broken them. As soon as the shelling had ceased a Brigade Signaller was ordered to carry out the necessary repairs, and as another man had to go with him for safety's sake, I volunteered for the job as I had not been into the village and wanted to see the results of the shelling.

We crawled along by the side of the wires, keeping below the level of the hedge, (for we were well within the range of being seen, and bullets were plentiful), and eventually found the break, and mended it.

We then walked round the church, and the first thing that came to one's notice, was a large crucifix on the outside wall, which had escaped without damage. The wall at one end was completely down, and at the other end were gaping holes where shells had passed through. Near the centre was the porch with the tower above and on the wall by the side, was a crucifix about ten feet long by some six feet wide, and the wall behind this crucifix was absolutely undamaged, although the wall on the other side of the church as well as the entire roof, was razed to the ground.

We then looked around the cemetery, and saw many graves opened by shellfire, bones, wood of coffins, tomb stones smashed, but noticed that several tomb stones made in the form of a crucifix, although the stone work comprising the cross had been damaged by shrapnel, the figure was still intact and un-hit.

The Brigade Signaller with me as regards religion was "nothing" although designated for Army purposes as "Church of England" but he also remarked on the wonderful preservation of the crucifix, and mentioned to me, that although he had not been to church for many years, beyond attending church parades "there must be something in it", and we enjoyed, on our way back, quite an interesting religious talk and it is very likely that good may result to both of us by what we saw this evening. One realised at this time how true is the expression "God's ways are not as our ways".

5.7.1915

The shelling was continuous on Monday the 5th July, and as my "dug-out" was not proof against shrapnel, I set to work to reconstruct it, and placed about three feet of earth on top as I did not want to finish my existence one night whilst asleep.

6.7.1915

Early in the morning of Tuesday the 6th July, the British on our left made a very determined attack, and succeeded in obtaining one line of Germ trenches. The Germs counter-attacked at 10.30am, and got their trenches back, and also attacked the line immediately in front of us. We "stood to" ready to go into the engagement at once. The Bosches in front of us, however, were repulsed, and we stayed where we were.

Through field glasses, I watched the enemy charge, which, although risky, was a sight I would not have missed on any account. It is seldom one gets such a position as behind a hedge from which to watch an attack at close quarters, and without such protection it would be madness to try and see the charge. When an enemy is advancing, and one is in the fire trench, one cannot take in the scene as one is about to fight for life, but being in the second line, with so much protection, gave me the opportunity.

With Major Cohen[33] (our Senior Major) I watched the Bosches advancing and falling dead or wounded from our rifle and machine gun fire, and hardly a man reached our front line.

The length of the bombardment had not been sufficient to kill very many of our men, and there were plenty left to repel this attack.

At any minute we were prepared to counter-charge should the Germs succeed in penetrating our line but we were not wanted, for the fire trench was like a wall of steel, against which nothing could prevail.

Later in the day, the regiments on our left again attacked and took the line of trenches, which constituted the original attack and evening fell with us in possession.

7.7.1915

We "stood to" early in the morning of Wednesday the 7th July, as the Germs counter-attacked very fiercely on the left, but they did not succeed in breaking the line. In the evening I went to La Brique for rations as usual, and the firing was fairly heavy.

8.7.1915

Again the Germs attacked in front of us, morning and evening of Thursday the 8th July, but in each case they were easily repulsed. The firing was terrific especially at the evening attack, and the sight of the bursting shells, which we watched through a gap in the hedge, was most appalling, even if rather uncomfortable when the shells came near.

Although I was "cook", and thereby relieved of all duties on the wire, I offered to do a couple of hours for another man, from 4.00pm until 6.00pm as he had had a heavy day on account of the attacks. I "came off" at 6.00pm and about 10 minutes later the Germs started shelling us with the "salvos" (four or six shells at a time) which fell all around the Signal Office. The shelling was so severe that we all had to "clear out" to the communication trenches (which is permitted in any trench but the front line if the shelling is very heavy, but of course if an attack is made on the fire trench, we would all have to return to our posts) with the exception of two

---

[33] Now Colonel; since died.

Signallers who must on no account leave while instruments can be worked.

As a matter of fact, all the wires were broken, and the Signallers left their office to report to the commanding officer that communication had been stopped. They had no sooner got clear when a couple of shells landed - one in the Signal Office, and the other in an officers' "dug-out" a couple of yards away. We kept clear for about half an hour, and then returned to our posts.

We then saw some very peculiar sights. A rifle in the Signal Office had been twisted in a most peculiar manner, such as one might find a candle on a hot day. (It was suggested to use the rifle for shooting around corners.) Everything was scattered about the office, and the roof had completely fallen in, covering everything with dirt.

The "dug-out" next door had suffered in a similar manner. The officer who occupied it, happened to have a shelf on which had been placed a pair of socks. On another shelf had been a drinking mug. We found the mug bent and battered, holding firmly in its mouth the pair of socks so tightly, that it would be impossible to pull them out without tearing them. This "souvenir" was sent to England.

9.7.1915

During the afternoon of Friday the 9th July, I cut a short sap from my "buggy" (which was in front of the others some short distance) to a communication trench in rear, along which to travel instead of walking over the top. Last evening I had had to "double" over open ground, in view of the Germs, when the shelling started, and I considered it was "not good enough".

10.7.1915

On Saturday the 10th July, the Germs gave us plenty of "hate" and in the evening made another very determined attack on our left, and it was so serious that for safety's sake, it was decided that the "trench log book" should be sent to Brigade Headquarters about a mile back on the canal bank.

I had just returned from La Brique with the ration cart, and was about to "turn in", when I was called up at 11.15pm, to take the book to Brigade on foot, my bicycle having been smashed by a shell some time ago.

I had prepared for my night's sleep (which is not allowed) and my preparations consisted of taking off my respirator, and using it as a pillow.

As every man was wanted in the trench in case of casualties, I was ordered to go by myself, so I put on my coat, and saw that my rifle was in good working order, and in the hurry and urgency of the matter, forgot all about my respirator (gas mask).

In blissful ignorance, I traversed the fields in the rear of the trenches, keeping behind a hedge as very heavy firing was in progress, and got to the road, when suddenly I sniffed GAS, and I had no respirator! What was I to do? I dared not go back to the trenches as I would be going further into the gas area, and would very likely be overcome before reaching my "dug-out". I decided to hurry along; get to La Brique; and see if I could get a spare one there.

The further I advanced, the stronger the smell, which seemed strange to me and not like the gas we had smelt before, but a more familiar smell and at last I began to get the "wind up", and wondered what length of time I had to live, and why the distance to La Brique seemed so long.

Suddenly I heard a gentle purr and ahead I saw the outline of a cart. The smell grew stronger but perhaps help in the direction of a respirator was near at hand. At the same time, why was the smell getting so pronounced, especially as the wind was in front of me? Surely I was getting along quicker than the gas.

Suddenly the mystery was solved. It was not gas I could smell, but the fumes of about a dozen motor ambulances which had arrived ready to take the wounded to hospital, and they were all ready to move off, and emitting petrol fumes from the exhaust.

I cannot say that usually I enjoy the fumes of motor cars, which often spoil the sweet scents of the countryside in dear old England, but on this occasion nothing could have been sweeter.

I was so pleased with the smell, that I gave a sincere sigh of relief and contentment, and then realised for the first time that the pathway across the fields along which I had to go was being shelled, and also the fields in the rear by the canal bank.

I tried to obtain a respirator, but no one had a spare one, so I would not wait for the shelling to cease, in case gas was in reality sent over, which was more than likely. With another man on the same errand as I, from another Battalion, I started to cross. This other man did not know his way, and would not risk it by himself, but on my stating that I would not wait he "fell in" with me.

Every two or three minutes we had to throw ourselves to the ground as we heard a shell coming near,[34] and suddenly a few yards in front of us there were four brilliant flashes and deafening reports. We dared not move, for we were practically stunned. I then remembered that there was a battery of artillery in the field, and discovered that we were walking straight towards the guns![35]

It was a very black night, and the brilliant flashes had made it practically impossible to see at all. We crawled along shouting: "Battery, are you there?" "Friends here," or some such remark, when we were halted by a guard and taken to a "dug-out" where there was an artillery officer.

He told us to rest and asked our business. On our informing him that we were taking the log to Brigade, he said we could not go on as they were shelling all-round the Brigade Headquarters.

He asked us from where we had come, and when we told him "across the fields in front," he would hardly believe us, he said that it was impossible to live through such a bombardment as the fields had had. He told us that the Germs were trying to silence his guns, and that it was very dangerous here (very cheerful), and all he dared do, was to go out occasionally and fire his guns, and then return at once with all his men to the "dug-out".

We waited in the "dug-out", during which time he obtained for me a respirator (which put my mind at rest), and we then had a chat about my regiment, in which he was interested as his grandfather, or somebody, had once belonged to it. After about half an hour, the Germs transferred their attention to other directions, and we were allowed to proceed.

We found on arriving at Brigade Headquarters that the shelling was still going on, so we decided to get to the Signal Office quickly, which was across the bank of the canal, and get under cover there. We got there and found the General and his staff sitting on biscuit tins as their "dug-out" had been smashed, so we sat in there for about half an hour and heard all the news as to the progress of the

---

[34] If you hear a shell, it has passed but it is natural to duck.
[35] Safe – fire up in the air but not nice.

attack as it came through over the wire, finishing with a message to the effect that the "Germs just attacked and repulsed".

As things were now quieter the General (General Congreve VC)[36] told us we could get back to our units and I eventually arrived in my little "buggy" about 3.00am after reporting to the commanding officer, who asked me if I had had a "good time", and saying that he honestly did not expect I would have got through.

11.7.1915

During the evening of Sunday the 11th July, we were relieved by the Leicestershire Regiment, after a very trying period of 17 days in the trenches.

The Signallers were relieved a couple of hours before the rest of the Battalion, and we got to the huts between Vlamertinghe and Poperinghe and "turned in", and were well asleep before the remainder of the Battalion arrived.

The return from the trenches is especially looked forward to by the Signallers, for the section becomes like a large family, and in the trenches we are separated and posted for duty, two or three at a certain station, whereas the companies are of course always together. The nights on which we come out of the trenches are invariably very noisy amongst the Signallers, for we would all tell our various experiences at the same time, one to another. We consequently used to get into much trouble from the "'eads" nearby, who perchance might desire to repose. However, in spite of the fact that we were always getting "jawed", they could not do without their Signallers, if only for the reason that there would be nobody else to cause trouble.

12.7.1915

On Monday the 12th July we had a general clean up, and inspections of kit etc. I did duty on the wire from 4.00pm until 8.00pm; my duties as cook having terminated. We got a draft from England of about 300 men, as we had lost so many lately and the strength of the Battalion was again very low.

---

[36] General Congreve VC. Died Gibraltar.

13.7.1915

We were up at 6.30am on Tuesday the 13th July, and paraded for physical drill. Later in the morning we had "buzzer" and heliograph practice. Rather a funny incident was the result of the helio work we did, and it was this way.

With a helio it is possible to send messages many miles, as long as the sun is bright, and we saw a long distance off what we took to be a Germ captive balloon. We began to send messages to the balloon which were far from complimentary in character, and when we packed up we felt very pleased with our morning's work. We had to keep very quiet, however, when during the afternoon a message was received by all units and local Battalions to the effect that "during the morning, a heliograph had been fixed on to one of our captive balloons, and objectionable messages sent by some person or persons unknown" and requesting that every effort be made to trace those responsible.

With Rifleman R. Head,[37] on completion of our morning's industry, I went to Poperinghe, and we had a good dinner at an Estaminet, and made a number of purchases.

We returned in an empty motor lorry, and bumped all along the cobbled road from "Pop" to "Vlam", and we were by no means sorry when the journey came to an end.

14.7.1915

Physical drill again at 6.30am on Wednesday the 14th July, and afterwards duty as the Battalion Cyclist during the morning, which necessitated two journeys to Brigade Headquarters in Poperinghe.

In the afternoon I again went to Poperinghe with Riflemen Rolfe, and had a bath. Rolfe bought a luminous watch in Poperinghe, and as he wished to dispose of the one he had, I bought it for 10 francs.

I therefore had mine to sell, and on putting it up for auction I got three francs for it, which considering I bought it for rough usage and originally paid 2/9d for it, was not so bad, especially as I had had it for nine months, and the glass was cracked. But then in France watches were very dear, and it really was a good time-keeper.

---

[37] Met in Epsom Hospital.

15.7.1915

St Swithin's Day, Thursday the 15th July, was the occasion for more "physical jerks", and afterwards clothes washing (much needed).

I was on duty on the wire from 4.00pm until 8.00pm, and then attended a concert which had been got up by members of the Q.W.R.

16.7.1915

On Friday the 16th July, we practised a system whereby we might be able to "tap" the Germs' telegraph wires. I might mention that we made sure that the system would not work, especially as it meant a Signaller going "over the top", as near the Germs' lines as possible.[38]

17.7.1915

We had a day off on Saturday the 17th July on account of heavy rainfall. In the evening we held another excellent concert in the open. The Q.W.R. were not daunted by the rain which fell all the time.

18.7.1915

Sunday morning the 18th July, I attended at Mass in a field nearby, and in the afternoon was on duty from 4.00pm until 8.00pm.

19.7.1915

At 3.00pm on Monday the 19th July, we left once more for the trenches, and at 6.30pm reached Potiejze Wood without too much excitement. We had just arrived in the wood when the British at Hooge (300 to 400 yards on our right) blew up a mine, which is now so famous, and where so many have since lost their lives, called the "crater at Hooge"; and as this was the first big mine we had seen so clearly we were astonished, and at first did not know what to make of it. There was a tremendous report, the earth shook, and a voluminous mass of smoke floated upwards.

---

[38] Major Cohen's idea.

We then opened up with our artillery, and all the guns around were firing, causing a great deal of noise, and in the distance was a line of flame and smoke from the shells bursting over the Germs' line. A charge was then made, and the British succeeded in obtaining the positions which they were after.

Soon, the Germs recovered from the surprise of the attack, and began to bombard our line very severely, and the men in the British fire trench suffered very large casualties.

There was a Wireless Station in the wood, and after the Germs' bombardment had been going on for some time, we had been watching it from positions behind walls, trees, etc., we were ordered to get into "dug-outs" at once, as a shelling of the wood was imminent.

The "dug-outs" were splendidly made, and had a thickness of some five to six feet of earth on top, and were proof against shrapnel. We had no sooner squeezed in when the Germs commenced a violent cannonade of shrapnel shells. We were then told that our Wireless Station had sent out a message in Germ, as follows: "British infantry amassing in Potiejze Wood", and this message had been picked up by the Germs, and they had taken their fire off the trenches and shelled the wood. Except for the men in the "dug-out" there was nobody in the wood, so no damage was done. The Wireless Station of course knew that only shrapnel would be fired, for slaughtering infantry en masse, and also firing into a wood, high explosive percussion shells would not be used.

We had about two hours of this bombardment, and then evidently the Germs discovered the trick and stopped shelling, and again fired on the trenches, but by this time it had given our men in the firing line a chance to recover. I expect the Germs were pleased with themselves for having been "taken in".

I had a chat with the priest[39] attached to the Leinster Regiment who had just come from the trenches and he told me very many interesting anecdotes of a religious character connected with his regiment, and then, with another Signaller, I proceeded to relieve the Leinster Signallers.

---

[39] ? Father Cooter.

20.7.1915

The companies did not arrive until half an hour after midnight on Tuesday the 20th July. After putting the Company to which I was attached in their portion of the trench (which was on the left of the Menin Road, and a few hundred yards from Hooge), I went on duty on the wire until 3.00am.

The position of the trench which we occupied was as "lively" a spot as I encountered around the salient, and we had an awful number of casualties.

I will shortly be introducing "Stink Cottages", and to give an idea of this "health resort", I will mention the number of casualties daily out of 20 men who had to be there.

We were some 700 yards from the Germs, and about 50 or 60 yards in front of our line were two or three houses, with large gardens attached. Having heard that there was a good supply of new potatoes growing, I decided that the only way to obtain possession of them was to go "over the top" as evening was beginning to fall, take a sack, and dig them up. I made up my mind to do this, and about 8.00pm I went over, and got about half way across, when an attack commenced at Hooge. I "carried on", however, and got to the houses. I was gathering a large number of "spuds", when the Germs took it into their heads to commence shelling, some of which shells fell within 10 or 20 yards from me, between the trenches and myself. I decided that this spot was not too healthy, so I threw my sack across my back, and "doubled" across to the trenches, making a mental note to myself that I would go without potatoes in future, rather than fetch them in this manner.

The Germs made a bombing attack about this time at "Stink Cottages", and we had one man killed, and several wounded.

21.7.1915

On Wednesday the 21st July, our Adjutant (Captain Flower), of the K.R.R.C, left the Regiment on being promoted to the rank of Brigade Major, and in him we lost an officer who did excellent work in keeping the Battalion together. As can be readily understood the duty on the wire during the night was by no means the most congenial and I was very surprised when the Signaller at the Station with me suggested that I should do duty on the wire during the day, and he would take all the night work. I readily fell in with the suggestion and discovered after about a week that his principle of doing night duty was quite peculiar to himself. I came off duty at 10.00pm and he would do a couple of hours' duty and put the instrument around his head and "turn in", and not wake up until about eight o'clock next morning. Luckily for him he was not found out, but I could quite understand why he proposed night duty as in these conditions it was not very tedious or a great strain.

In the evening there was plenty of artillery round our way and another small attack at "Stink Cottages." Consequent to this attack we had about eight casualties.

22.7.1915

At 7.00am on Thursday the 22nd July, the Germs attacked and bombed "Stink Cottages" but, on this occasion, our men evacuated the position and took cover at a spot about 20 yards behind and when the bombing was over again, advanced to the sap by "Stink Cottages" and gave the Germs a supply of bombs with interest. By this means we managed to avoid casualties. There was much rain during the day and the trenches were practically waterlogged. In the evening I went across to the "White Chateau" in Potiejze Wood and drew a few extra rations. There was a great deal of shelling going on which re-echoed right through the Potiejze Wood causing a tremendous amount of noise. The casualties at "Stink Cottages" this day amounted to one killed and four or five wounded.

23.7.1915

Friday the 23rd July was quite like a day in April being at times very fine and at others very showery. The casualties this day at "Stink Cottages" were four men killed, which included the champion boxer[40] of the London Banks.

24.7.1915

At 6.00am on a Saturday the 24th July, the Germs without any consideration of our feelings heavily shelled our trench and disturbed my peaceful slumbers. One shell, which fell about 20 yards from me, wounded five men.

---

[40] Bell Chambers.

"Stink Cottages" again came in for a bombardment, this time with trench mortars and aerial torpedoes, but no casualties were caused on this occasion.

There was a fair sized farm just behind the Germs' line which we designated "Krupp's Farm". In the evening one of our star shells fell on some inflammable material in the farm and set fire to the premises. The light from the fire, which necessarily had to run its course, was very brilliant and lit up the whole countryside. We were by that means able very often to spot the enemy bringing up his rations, working parties, etc. and there is no doubt many of them carried rations for the last time. Apart from this, it was a very fine sight seeing the farm one mass of flame.

Casualties at "Stink Cottages" this day were one killed and three wounded.

25.7.1915

Sunday the 25th July was indeed an ideal day and like many other Sundays the firing was not very intense. In the evening I witnessed a sight which was as splendid a display of aircraft strategy I have seen. It came about as follows: It is usual as evening is drawing to a close for patrolling aeroplanes of both the British and Germs to go up high behind their own lines to observe the movement of troops and transport that necessarily take place when dusk is falling. It is very seldom that these machines, which are of a heavy type, go beyond their own lines or attempt battle.

Suddenly one of our machines left its course and went straight towards the Germs' lines. Three Germs' machines came forward ready to offer resistance. Our aeroplane still went forward and the Germs closed in to attack. Our machine quickly turned tail and retreated, and we below were watching and could not understand the idea at all, when out of the clouds we saw a monoplane above the Germs' machines, which our aeroplane had drawn on. The monoplane dropped a bomb,[41] which caught one of the Taubes. The two Germs' machines turned tail and retreated and the other burst into a mass of flame and began falling to the ground.

At the same time there rang out from the British trenches a tremendous cheer and the Germans opened up a rapid fire.

---

[41] Or machine gunned.

Unfortunately one of our men got rather too excited and had his head above the parapet and was instantly killed.

The observer inside the blazing Germ machine tumbled out and fell between the lines. The pilot made a splendid attempt to land and we did not fire at him, as he was going in our direction so gave him a chance. He was, however, not content and made an effort to turn his machine round to make for his own line and we opened fire at him, but it is doubtful if he was touched. It was all ended in the space of a few seconds when the machine turned turtle and dived to earth, falling behind our trenches. Both machine and pilot were burnt to cinders.

> You do not hear much about the discomforts of life up in the trenches. Men will grouse about being short of timber for strengthening the dug-outs or this and that, but you seldom hear a word about the real hardships, the difficulty of getting a proper wash, the ceaseless strain, the flies, the hundred and one discomforts which are inseparable from this unprecedented war of positions.
>
> The other day I was in a position which is less than thirty yards from the German trenches, where the few men holding the place squat doubled up in a narrow trench with a stack of bombs at hand to repel an attack. The trench runs through some ruined buildings, where the dead of many months are lying, some buried in the soil through which our trenches run, others entombed beneath piles of loose bricks.
>
> I sat down on the ground beside the Irishmen, who were in that foul place, and chatted with them. In a piece of mirror stuck up on the parados, I could see the German trench at a distance considerably less than the width of the Strand at its narrowest point. "There's an Alleman that comes out of the trinch once again," they said to me in horse whispers. "Sure an we often see him pattering about, a gran big fellow with great whiskers on him. 'Tis a pity not to shoot him. We could get him every time."
>
> I touched the mirror to move it. The next instant two bullets struck the sandbags on the parados on either side of the glass. The men laughed. "They can't hit you the way you have your head now, sorr," they said, "but don't be raisin yourself."
>
> Hours of ceaseless watching in that narrow, cramped-up space, with death the penalty for an unreflecting movement, roasted by the sun, pestered by flies—this was the daily portion of these gentle, gallant Irishmen, who hated the German

33. Report from an Irish Soldier

About 10 minutes after, a Germ aeroplane appeared flying very low right behind our trenches in order to spot where the machine had fallen with the object of destroying any documents or papers of value which might be in the machine. Our artillery did not fire a shot at this aeroplane, but after a few minutes the Germs commenced a heavy shelling round the spot where the aeroplane had fallen.

It was now my turn for duty at "STINK COTTAGES". The name of "STINK COTTAGES" was indeed well earned, for the position consisted of about five or six cottages which ran at the side of the communication trench from our lines to the Germs' line. This communication trench was most important, for at one time the trenches in which the Germs were belonged to us, and they took them from us when the gas attack was made in April.

It was necessary to make sure that the Germs did not have possession of these cottages as it would have given them a position whereby they could fire into our trenches on the heads of our men. We therefore defended the communication trench right up to these cottages, when it was blocked up by refuse, dead bodies etc. for a space of 15 yards, the other side of the barrier being used by the Germs as their advance listening post. As will be seen from the sketch below, on account of the importance of the position the Germs kept making attacks, but we still retained the position.

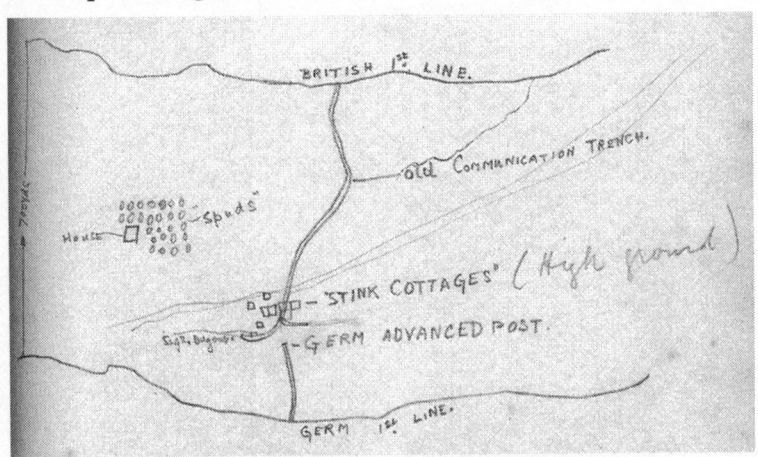

34. Sketch of Position of Stink Cottages

The strain at this point was so severe that 24 hours was the greatest length of time for any man to be there.

Every evening 20 men would be detailed to hold this sap for the night, and it was impossible to get along the sap during the day. Two Signallers went up every night with the 20 men. There was only one "dug-out" of a very disreputable character, which was used by the Signallers. When this "dug-out" was made, the digging party came across what was a woman buried in all her clothes. Evidently she had been killed when the cottages were shelled. There was a leg with a boot on which penetrated one wall of the "dug-out" and it served as a table on which to work the instruments.

The height of the trench was no more than three feet and one could never stand up nor do any work at all during the day or night to improve the position.

At about 8.30pm with my chum, I crawled along the four or five hundred yards to "Stink Cottages" and relieved the Signallers who had been on during the last 24 hours. One of them who was about my own age, had suffered so terribly from the strain, that his hair in parts, had turned quite white, and after his return from the trenches, he[42] eventually got to England.

We took over and telegraphed through to Headquarters that we had arrived. The rest of the men were relieved one by one, and during this process, four men paid the penalty.

It was forbidden to strike matches but I managed by lighting my pipe in the "dug-out" to set all the men smoking, taking lights from one another's cigarette.

26.7.1915

All night long continual fire at point-blank range was carried out by the Germs and the noise was absolutely deafening, and of course we got no sleep.

We got a number of bombs over but no attack was made.

During the day two men were killed and three wounded, and they had to stay in the trench until night time before they could be removed.

Apart from the strain which these 24 hours had, I must say it was the worst time I have ever experienced in my life. The atmosphere was terrible.

Just at the side of the sap was a dead horse, and the warmth of the weather had made the stench from the number of dead lying

---

[42] Rifleman Buckley.

around most objectionable. I was indeed thankful when at about 8.00pm we were relieved by two Signallers from the Sherwood Foresters,[43] and proceeded to the Chateau in Potiejze Wood where we met the rest of the Signallers who were anxiously waiting our return.

We were detailed to go to the billets on the northern outskirts of Ypres, and the Battalion were to do fatigues for other regiments in the trenches. Ypres, however, was being so badly shelled by "woolly bears" that we had to wait for some considerable time before we dare risk going through the town. Eventually however we went across some fields and got to our billet about midnight.

We were now about two miles from the trenches and were in houses, which were more or less battered by shellfire. To make ourselves comfortable before turning in, we went to some houses near the "Water Tower" and obtained a supply of mattresses more or less clean. We marched proudly along the road with these mattresses on our backs and laid them down preparatory to "turning in". We "tossed up" for duty and I lost, so had to go on the wire until 4.00am.

27.7.1915

On Tuesday the 27th July, after duty I had what I considered a well-earned sleep after a period of over 40 hours without sleep.

In the evening the Germs were thoughtful enough to send over a supply of gas which reached us in a large quantity, and necessitated us wearing our smoke helmets. The only "military" damage they achieved however, was to deprive us of smoking for an hour or two.

After the "wind" fell I went for a short walk and came back when we had a "singsong", to the annoyance of the sergeant major who resided next door. As sergeant majors never swear however, no doubt no harm resulted from this very enjoyable evening.

28.7.1915

I washed some clothes on Wednesday the 28th July, and I really cannot say it wasn't necessary.

In the afternoon I was on duty from noon until 4.00pm, and the Germs again granted us another liberal supply of gas.

---

[43] We were lucky.

29.7.1915

I was on duty from 4.00am until 8.00am on Thursday the 29th July, and later on in the morning with two of my friends, "Dear and Chamberlain",[44] decided to take the risk of a trip around Ypres.

I might say that these two were of a very adventurous and daring spirit, and did not mind at all whether we were caught, which if had been the case when we were coming out of a house, if looting we would have been liable to be shot, in theory.

However, we got through a number of orchards, picking a very good supply of nice fruit (there being no owner to object) and crossed over the canal getting into one of the main streets of Ypres.

On our left we passed a big open space in which there were roundabouts, skittle alleys, such as may be seen at our English fairs, and everything as far as we could see was in working order, except for the fact that many of the parts were damaged by shells.

We made a very noble attempt to induce the roundabout to work but all our efforts in this direction were in vain. Even the barrel organ refused to give forth any melody.

However, we passed on our way[45] and in the street were gaping holes where shells had penetrated right down into the sewage drains. On the other side were houses smashed beyond recognition, and a little further along the road we came up to the Cathedral. There was no one in sight.

We went right inside the Cathedral and observed the bricks, masonry, glass and roofing piled high in an irregular heap of debris in the interior of the church. The roof was completely destroyed and the sky could be seen overhead. Many portions of the walls were demolished, also the sanctuary except for the crucifix which still stood behind the high altar looking down on the wreckage, and above the crucifix the roof was still intact.

We then proceeded to the Cloth Hall across the road and saw the paintings on the walls, which were terribly damaged and smothered in dust.

We obtained various "souvenirs" such as pieces of masonry etc., but unfortunately I was not able to bring them back with me to England.

---

[44] Dear since killed? Chamberlain killed.
[45] It was invariably by night that we went through Ypres.

We had been in Ypres now for some considerable time, and were forgetting that there was any risk of us being caught, when suddenly we heard the hoofs of horses going through Ypres. We looked about for a place to take cover and observed a number of niches from where the statues were removed, and we took the place of the saints, which had at one time occupied so prominent a position. Unfortunately we had all just lit our pipes and continued our smoke, which a lynx-eyed military policeman managed to spot and came round to investigate. On seeing us he remarked that we were as little like saints as he could imagine and proceeded to take our names. There was also a French military policeman with him, and we had a long discussion apologising and trying to explain that we did not know we could not go in to Ypres, etc. etc. The yarn I pitched in very broken French punctuated with scraps of English was no doubt very impressive for we heard nothing more about the matter, and were very fortunate and got off without any trouble.

There was a five-inch field gun in a field some 200 yards from our billets, and when it fired the percussion was so great that the house in which we were, shook violently.

In the evening with the same two Signallers I went and had a look at the gun when it was firing. The Germs began to reply so we hurriedly took to some "dug-outs" which were not far from the gun. We were greatly struck by the simplicity in which these guns were fired (on the lanyard principle) which to us seemed much more convenient than the way in which the ignition of a howitzer is made. In the evening we had another supply of gas, and after it had blown over we went out hunting for nose caps. We found some, but they were so tainted with the smell of gas that we did not take them away with us.

We then "found" a chicken which was anxiously looking for a home, and after mercifully wringing its neck, sat in a shell hole nearby, and commenced the very trying occupation of plucking its feathers. We also went into some fields nearby and "found" some peas and beans which we stuffed into our pockets, and with light hearts and under cover of darkness, retraced our steps towards home where we displayed our trophies making the rest of the section very envious.

We then turned in for the night.

30.7.1915

At 4.00am on Friday the 30th July, the Germs made a big attack at Hooge when they released the liquid fire, and thereby made the British retire from one line of trenches.

The shelling was very intense, and at the same time they gave Ypres an unusually severe bombardment.

We were all ordered up and went out into the field some distance away, and the Signallers had no sooner got out of their billets when the house next door was caught by a shell and completely razed to the ground. After half an hour we again returned to the billet and turned in.

Later on in the morning we cooked our well-won chicken, and it may be interesting as a recipe to enumerate the ingredients which we used in the process of stuffing.

We found in a cupboard in our house a quantity of flour, which had probably been there since the owners evacuated many months previously. I then suggested in the absence of anything better, that an apple cut up into small portions would be very tasty. This was agreed to by the Company, a pear soon followed, two greengages were then cut up, peas and beans chopped up into fragments were then added. Somebody brought in a rat and other similar refuse, but that, under no consideration would we permit to be added to our already voluminous supply, and both rat and owner were unceremoniously kicked out without regard for either's feelings.

Considering the size of the bird, which, to us, looked as if it had been on "short rations" for many months, the quantity of stuffing which we managed to get in was indeed very creditable. The Signal Section who were not partaking in the chicken said that this was accomplished by the fact that each man would pull its neck, and by that means give more space to put in the stuffing.

We boiled the chicken and partook of it at mid-day with new potatoes, beans and peas, followed up by stewed greengages which was greatly enjoyed.

During the afternoon there was another attack at Hooge and we were again shelled out of our billets, so to get out of the way, we went to an Estaminet[46] not far from the guns, where we were entertained very socially by three nice little girls who were still there selling "milk" to the troops.

---

[46] ? About 3 miles behind the lines.

I was on duty from 8.00pm until midnight.

31.7.1915

We got up at eight o'clock after a night of heavy bombardment, but we did not leave our billets as the shells were not so near as they were the night before. The shelling however, for the past day or so had been very intense.

In the evening we were ordered to dig some trenches not far from our billets, to which we were immediately to proceed in the event of our billets being shelled. At nine o'clock in the evening there was another attack at Hooge and we were ordered to "stand to", ready to go into the battle, but by midnight we got orders that we were not required, and were therefore able to partake of our repose.

35. Sketch of Author

1.8.1915

On Sunday the 1st August, things were a bit quieter and we had a general clean-up.

During the afternoon the Germs shelled us very heavily with six-inch shrapnel and gas shells, and as we had not completed our digging operations, we had to take to the cellars which were available.

2.8.1915

On Monday the 2nd August, we had a very liberal supply of shells at our billets. We got orders during the afternoon that we were to leave Ypres and go to Poperinghe, and at 6.30pm proceeded on our way past the water tower, gaol and asylum, and got on the road to Vlamertinghe.

I might here mention the wonderful defences which were between Ypres and Vlamertinghe, the details of which, although interesting, I must refrain from stating for obvious reasons.

On the road three or four of us stopped at an Estaminet and partook of a certain amount of "joy water", and we got detached from the rest of the Signal Section. They however, had left us the truck in which were the Signallers' instruments, and we had to push it all the way to Poperinghe.

It was a very dark night and rain was beginning to fall and when we got to Poperinghe, in order to find the rest of the section we used Signalling lamps, sending our "Q.W.R" call, thereby getting into trouble with the military police who came over in a rush to see who was Signalling.

Eventually we found the rest of the section and took up our billets in a convent in which there were quite a number of the sisters of the order of "Petite Soeurs des Pauvres".

We eventually turned in about 10.30pm.

3.8.1915

We got up about nine o'clock on Tuesday the 3rd August, and the air was full of rumours.

The first rumour that came through was that we were going to leave the Ypres district, hence our going to Poperinghe. Later it was rumoured that we had got a few days' rest preparatory to going into a big attack and this latter proved to be true.

Nothing very exciting happened today, and we finished up with a convivial evening at an Estaminet where one was able to get bottles of very good Champagne for the moderate sum of three and a half francs.

In this town we were able also to get the Belgian shag tobacco, 18 sous a pound, and first class cigars for two sous. The Belgian tobacco I, personally, rather liked once I'd got used to it, but the French tobacco I could not stick at any price. However, as we were issued with English tobacco as a ration, I did not often take advantage of the Belgian shag.

We turned in at ten o'clock and during the night the town was very heavily shelled.

4.8.1915

On Wednesday the 4th August, with my chum Dear (whom I am sorry to say has recently been reported "missing"),[47] I went round and had a look at the damage which had been done, which, considering the ferocity of the bombardment, was not very excessive.

We went inside one of the churches in Poperinghe, which had been slightly damaged, and there was as beautiful an old carved pulpit as I have ever seen. It was a great height and all hand carved, and I was told that it was nearly 1,000 years old.

We had dinner out and finished up the day with another convivial evening.

5.8.1915

On Thursday the 5th August, we had orders to prepare for a journey to Ypres. During the day the General commanding our Brigade called a parade of the D.L.I. and told them that they were to take back the trenches which had been lost by the attack with liquid fire on the 30th July, and said that the Queen's Westminster Rifles were going to be in support.

Both the Durhams and ourselves were very pleased to think that we were about to see the "real thing", and the expression used by the Commandant of the Durhams "that he desired no one else but the Queen's Westminsters to support him, to ensure the operation

---

[47] Since killed R.I.P.

being a success", was on a par with our feelings, "with the Durhams in front we had nothing to fear".

The relations between the Durham Light Infantry and the Queen's Westminster Rifles were most cordial.

We were due to leave at five o'clock in the evening when the Germs began to shell the road between Poperinghe and Vlamertinghe, and we had to delay our departure for a couple of hours.

The D.L.I. left at 6.30pm and we followed half an hour later. But unfortunately the Germs' aeroplanes observed the Durhams along the road and directed the Germs' battery's fire, and as a result eighteen men of the Durhams were killed and 22 wounded.

The Commandant of the Durhams had his horse shot from under him, but he, himself, escaped injury.

When we followed a little later we saw the result of the shelling and it was by no means a cheerful spectacle.

We continued on our way and as the shelling of the town was in progress, we kept to the side streets in the southern portion and I saw the only part of Ypres, which so far I had not yet seen.

Here, the havoc was very terrible, and I had a bicycle and went along in front of the Battalion in order to find the way through.

The moon was shining brightly and after going along a short way, I found it was impossible to cycle, so lifting my machine on my back, I continued on foot with two or three men, occasionally sending one back with the direction in which to proceed.

The roadway was piled high with bricks and debris, which had not been cleared away and a short distance in front I observed a tall, gaunt looking obstacle. I went forward and found that I had lost my way on the road, and was walking on what was left of the houses, and had come straight up to a wall, which was still standing. I therefore had to re-trace my steps and managed to find a better way, eventually arriving at the Ypres ramparts about eleven o'clock.

We were not going up to the trenches this night, but were to stay at the ramparts and go up on the morrow.

We relieved the K.O.Y.L.I, and then turned in about midnight.

6.8.1915

In preparation for this attack there had been for the past three or four days a shelling by many batteries around, for half an hour, commencing at 2.30am, in order to demoralise the Germs; and although we did not attack, it made them expect an attack, and thereby put their nerves at very high tension.

On Friday the 6th August, we had a good look round the portion of Ypres near the ramparts. There was a large monastery in which was a chapel[48] and a very fine organ, and as we had several musicians in our regiment there was a continual supply of, I am pleased to say, music of a sacred character. I had a good look round this monastery which had been severely damaged, and found many books of a most interesting nature. There were old registers of births, marriages, etc., dating back several hundred years and also a number of old books in French and Latin.

The church of St Jacques nearby had suffered as badly as the Cathedral, and was in a state of absolute ruin.

The ramparts, which in olden days would probably have been impregnable, had in many parts been badly damaged by shells, and in front of the ramparts there was a very wide moat running from the north of the town to the south. The ramparts themselves were lined with trenches, which had been cemented and were beautifully dry.

During the afternoon I went along to the houses in the rear of the ramparts, and spent quite an interesting time watching a man operating a wireless installation, which was in a very protected position in the ramparts.

In the evening we went on top of the ramparts, and viewed the battlefront from this splendid point of vantage.

The moon was shining on the moat and the Menin Road was about 100 yards or so away. The moon and stars reflected in the moat.

Looking at this and no further everything seemed very peaceful and beautiful.

However, out there, were the trenches with shells bursting over them, star shells continually lighting up the position. Men and transport could be seen moving along the road, and above all was the roar of the guns, the scream of the shells as they went over our heads, and in the midst of all this uproar, the metallic rat-a-tat of the deadly machine gun.

It was indeed a mixture of peace and strife.

---

[48] ? St Jacques.

7.8.1915

At 2.30am on Saturday the 7th August the usual bombardment took place and our artillery reported that they were not quite ready for the attack, so it was postponed for a day.

We therefore had another look round the town during the day and did nothing in particular.

8.8.1915

On Sunday morning the 8th August the usual bombardment was again carried out.

There was no opportunity of going to Mass so we hung about in expectant groups, as we were going up the line to take over in the evening.

We left the ramparts at ten o'clock at night, and after a very tedious journey with much waiting about before the relief was carried out, we arrived at Maple Copse at two o'clock on Monday the 9th August.

9.8.1915

If only the Germs had known there were thousands of troops in the open round Maple Copse and had they started a bombardment, they would have inflicted a terrific number of casualties.

About 2.30am I got my wire fixed up and Station opened with the aid of my chum Dear. We had just settled down when our artillery opened up a preliminary bombardment. I have seen and heard a number of bombardments[49] but never anything so severe as this. The papers reported afterwards that at this attack, for the first time we had what might be called a sufficient supply of ammunition. The Germs had also a plentiful supply and their barrage fire on our trenches was terrible, but our concentration of guns and shells outweighed the Germs, and the British were out that night to make the Germs pay dearly for the strip of land they gained by the liquid fire.

After three-quarters of an hour of this massacre our guns lifted their range and commenced a barrage of fire on the Germs' second line of trenches to keep back their reserves and the Durhams charged and gained the objective. At 4.00am the shelling was still

---

[49] All to no purpose.

very intense and our wounded were passing through Maple Copse in large numbers. One man of the D.L.I. was so terribly wounded that it was decided not to remove him and he was placed on a stretcher and put in our "dug-out" where he expired within a quarter of an hour or so.

We were then ordered to move forward and take up our first line of trenches, and the Commandant of the Queen's Westminsters, Major Cohen, the Adjutant and Dear and myself went forward, and took up our position in Sanctuary Wood.

Sanctuary Wood which is now so well known by name to those at home, resembles only very slightly a wood, for so many trees are down, and there are so many men there buried through the shelling, that it is really more like a cemetery than a wood. Two companies of the Westminsters went up to the Germs' trenches with bombs, and one of my best friends in the Company, a fellow named Ford was killed whilst crossing the Menin Road.

Twice during the morning I had to run "over the top" with messages to the captured trenches as all communication wires had been broken.

The "Germs" were "strafing" us with a vengeance, and although we had captured their positions, things were looking very black. The Germs' heavies were pounding our trenches from the front and from our rear, for the trenches around Hooge were in the shape of a horseshoe.

We were told by Major Cohen, before we went into this attack that there was only one gun about which we need have any fear, and that was the Germs' "seventeen incher" which they had somewhere behind Hill 60, a short distance on our right.

We were informed that our artillery thought they had the range of this gun, and before the attack commenced they were going to open fire and try to silence it. They were, however, unsuccessful, and this gun kept firing systematically the whole day, ploughing up the trenches and shaking the very earth. The shells coming through the air could be heard a long distance off, the roar of the shell gradually growing more intense as it approached the trenches, and then dirt, men, wood etc. were flung up in the air to a tremendous height of about 200-300 feet, although when one heard a shell it was safe.

There was practically nothing left of these fresh trenches as our artillery had pretty well knocked them to pieces, and all there was, was one mass of gaping holes. I had to go up twice with messages.

About noon a message was received from Headquarters that the trenches were to be held "at all costs", and this order had to be delivered in the captured lines. It was given to one Signaller but he never returned. Again the message was sent up an hour or so later, and again the Signaller failed to reach his objective.

The bombardment was still going on fiercely, when at about 3.00pm our Major came to me and said that as I knew the way, and had been across twice successfully, he wished me to make another trip and get the message through.

I started out "over the top" and a machine gun opened up, and I had no other option but to drop into a communication trench nearby which was filled with water and dead men.

In this communication trench lay the men of the K.R.Rs who had been caught up by the liquid fire a few days previously, and the three letters which they wear on the epaulets on the shoulder, will always be engraved on my mind.

The "17 inch" Gun was still firing and I went along this communication trench treading on anything that came in my way.

I was soaked to the skin and covered in mud, and I found it was impossible to continue along this trench. I therefore jumped out on top, and with my rifle smothered in mud and bayonet fixed, got within 10 to 12 yards of the captured trench. It was then that a salvo of shells burst just above my head and threw me very heavily to the ground but I was not hit. Some men in our trench spotted me and ran out to give me a hand into the trench.

As far as I remember, there were about half a dozen men left who were not wounded, and no officers at all.

I gave them the written message,[50] and as I had to get back and report that I had delivered my message, two men who had been wounded decided to come out with me, and as I was unable to walk by myself, gave me a hand back to my station.

They took me to the Major[51] and said that I had delivered my message, and we were all talking when another shell burst nearby, throwing a mass of dirt, wood etc. all over us.

---

[50] Not sure.
[51] Major Tyrill killed in action December 1915.

A Signaller's War

I was then taken out of the trenches,[52] and cannot say that I remember much more until travelling in an ambulance[53] to hospital in Vlamertinghe.

I was placed on a stretcher next to a number of wounded Germ prisoners who were in this first field hospital, and I stayed there for some time.

Later on I was wakened, and the orderly proceeded to arouse the Germs, and their nerves were so affected, that they both jumped up and commenced fighting. This so completely upset me, that it put the finishing touch, and I was from that time in a state of semi-consciousness and could not speak.

10.8.1915

I then remember being put in the hospital train in my damp and wet clothes, waking up during the day of Tuesday the 10th August, in a nice comfortable bed in a hospital, at Camiers near Etaples.

Thus I made my exit from Belgium into France.

36. Wounded British Soldiers

---

[52] Learnt since that I was buried under a mass of debris and base of skull struck with timber.
[53] Which I believe passed through Hazebrouck.

Chapter 5

France

From 10th August 1915 until 12th August 1915

My mind is rather hazy as to what took place during the two days I was in hospital in France. I remember that I was given a bath in bed, and in the clean sheets I felt very comfortable, it was the first time for a year that I had anything like comfort.

I remember the nurses, which at this stage seemed like ministering angels. The way in which they attended to me I shall never forget. I had not seen an Englishwoman for many, many months, and the tenderness and devotion which they showed was most kind.

Whether it was that which brought tears to my eyes or not, I cannot say, but, remember that I cried without ceasing, and could not stop myself.

12.8.1915

I remained in bed until at six o'clock in the morning, Thursday, August 12th, when I was placed in a stretcher and told that I was going to England that day. I was feeling much better and cannot remember more of the incidents which took place at this time.

I was then put in an ambulance which went to Camieres, four or five miles away and then put in a beautifully equipped hospital train which left about 8.30am and arrived at Calais about eleven o'clock.

I then set to work to enter up in my pocket diary as many of the incidents as I could remember from the time I went into the attack, until I arrived at Calais.

I embarked on the H.S. "Brighton" and left the shores of France at one o'clock. On our way we passed two or three French submarines and other vessels of war. I left my stretcher on the quay, as I felt that I could walk, and I very much wanted to get on my legs, and it was by this means I was fortunate enough to get to a hospital, about which I will state more later.

The journey across the Channel was very circuitous on account of mines, but eventually the crowd of eager anxious faces, staring for the sight of England were rewarded by the outline of the cliffs of Dover. We raised a cheer of the most heartfelt nature, and from this moment I felt better and began rapidly to mend.

I had, however, got very thin and weak, although in France I had got quite fat. We arrived at Dover at about three o'clock, and I heard that the men on the ship were going to three different hospitals, one in the Midlands, one in London, and one at Walmer which was only a few miles away.

I felt terribly fatigued and not at all up to the journey, and I was fortunate enough to be able to arrange that I should go to Walmer.

France has now been left behind and once more I have set foot on English soil. How many times whilst in the trenches, have I thought that I would never again see England.

Chapter 6

England

From 12th August 1915 until 31st December 1915

12.8.1915

At Dover we were met by private motor cars which I afterwards found were those of Lord Loreburn, Sir Arthur Woolerton and Sir Charles and Lady Sargant, the latter being the Commandant of the hospital to which I was taken, namely a Saint Anselm's V.A.D. Hospital, Walmer.

We had tea such as we had not partaken of for months and were then ordered to bed.

37. Lord Loreburn

A SIGNALLER'S WAR

38. St Anselm's

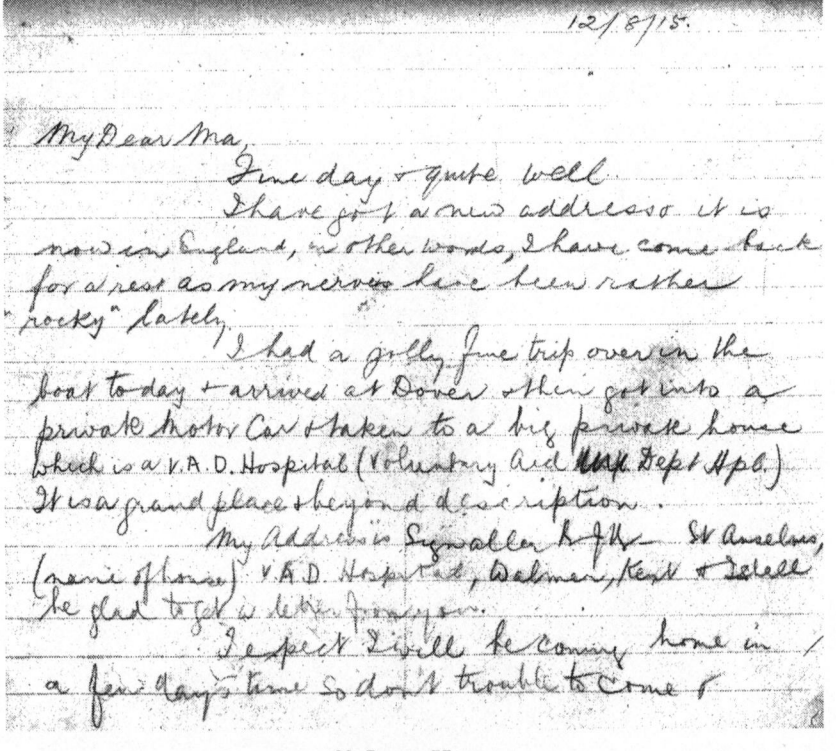

12/8/15.

My Dear Ma,

Fine day & quite well.

I have got a new address, it is now in England, in other words, I have come back for a rest as my nerves have been rather "rocky" lately.

I had a jolly fine trip over in the boat to-day & arrived at Dover & then got into a private motor car & taken to a big private house which is a V.A.D. Hospital (Voluntary Aid *** Dept HpL.) It is a grand place & beyond description.

My address is Signaller L. Jk— St Anselms, (name of house) V.A.D. Hospital, Walmer, Kent & I shall be glad to get a letter from you.

I expect I will be coming home in a few days time so don't trouble to come &

39. Letter Home

160

13.8.1915

I was in bed all Friday 13th August 1915 and managed to get up during the afternoon for a nice warm bath.

14.8.1915

Saturday 14th August was a beautiful day, and in at the afternoon I was allowed to get out and go in the grounds where I was initiated in the game of bowls.

40. Neurasthenia Report

15.8.1915

On Sunday 15th August I got up early in the morning, but was not allowed to go out or go to Church.

In the afternoon, however, with Sir Charles Sargant and a number of men, I went out for a quiet stroll down to the beach at Deal and there met many civilians and had a chat; and they were most kind to us and gave us many little things, such as cigarettes and tobacco, of which we were in need.

I could not help thinking how very strange that less than a week before I was in the most terrible part of the line in Flanders and only a few days ago in the midst of a raging battle, but now I was in England at the seaside where all was peace and quietness.

I remained in hospital for some weeks, during which time my mother, sisters, brothers (including one who is at present in France having been there nearly 15 months and just had leave), and many of my friends, paid me a visit.

SPORTS.

MORNINGSIDE, KINGSDOWN, DEAL.

Wednesday, August 18th, 1915.

2 O'CLOCK.

2.15. THREE-LEGGED RACE
  2 Prizes

2.45. EGG AND SPOON RACE
  1st Prize

3.15. CHILDREN'S RACE

3.30. APPLE RACE.
  1st Prize

4.0. HAT-TRIMMING COMPETITION.
  1st Prize

4.30. CUTTING THE CAKE.

5.0. TEA.

41. Sports' Day

17.8.1915

On Tuesday 17th August, Sir Robert Borden, (Prime Minister of Canada), visited the hospital and made a speech at dinner.

The patients in hospital had very many enjoyable afternoons and some very pleasant motor drives, walks, cricket matches and entertainments were provided by several of the local celebrities including Lord Loreburn, Sir Arthur Woolerton, Lady Hamilton (of Deal Castle), Lady Matthews and many others.

We also often went to the theatre at Deal and had excellent concerts in the hospital itself, and a band played weekly in our grounds, and everything was done that could be for our comfort.

Many amusing competitions were held such as trimming a ladies' hat, etc., and I was twice successful in obtaining the first prize in these competitions.

22.8.1915

On Sunday 22nd August my brother Fred[54] came to see me, and in the afternoon went over Deal Castle with me at the invitation of Lady Hamilton. The underground passages were very continuous and it was quite easy for one to get lost in them.

42. St Anselm's Reception Room

---

[54] Since killed in action R.I.P.

9.9.1915

Quite a peculiar fishing competition for the wounded soldiers was held on Thursday 9th September from Deal pier, in which every partaker received a prize.

I was fortunate enough to induce on to the end of my line two starfish and a crab, thereby obtaining a very nice box of handkerchiefs.

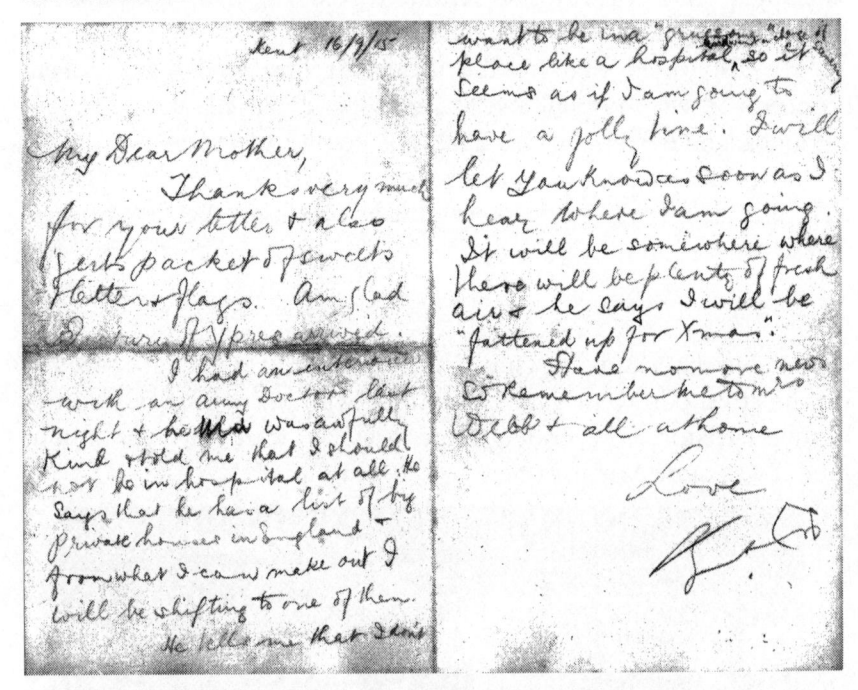

43. Letter from Convalescence

23.9.1915

On Thursday the 23rd September, Sir Arthur Woolerton took a party of us over Walmer Castle, which was most interesting. Incidentally we saw the room in which the Duke of Wellington died.

44. Patients in St Anselm's

24.9.1915

During the night two ships had been torpedoed just off the coast, and on Friday the 24th September we observed the result. One of the ships was carrying oil, which escaped, and for a large expanse the sea was absolutely "as smooth as a mill pond", and the odour from the oil was very strong. The smoothness of the sea where the oil was floating made it possible for one to imagine how the sea was calmed some years ago when the S.S. "Volturno" was sinking during a heavy storm in the Atlantic, and by this means many lives were saved.

> **"Carry On."**
>
> IN A V.A.D. hospital at meals the commandant, or one of the senior nurses, always has to say grace. One day there happened to be only one of the newest and shyest nurses at a certain hospital to do it, so she appealed to one of the sergeants to help her out. He consented, and, standing up, roared out, "Carry on."

45. St Anselm's Hospital Grace

St. ANSELM'S HOSPITAL ALPHABET.

A is for *Anselm*, our very own Saint,
Invoke him for help if you've any complaint.

B is for *Bandages*, skilfully plied,
Jack Johnson's and shrapnel fomenting inside.
If you're bandaged up well, and have borne the brunt,
You are sure to get asked if you're "back from the front?"

C for the *Concert*—each artiste a "Star"!
For our cricketers, too, who "Invincibles" are.

D is for *Dinner*, event of the day!
"Look out, if you please, stand clear of my tray!"
"Pass along there, now move down, please,
So the one-armed men may sit with ease."
"Who wants mince, and who wants fish?"
(I'm sure to forget which it is they wish).
"Coming up! Coming up!" "Second helpings, please,"
"Don't pour the rice on the patients' knees!"

E is for *Elegance*. When asked out to tea,
The polish on boots is a marvel to see!

F is for *Fishing*—though there's no sign of fish—
Still, starfish and crabs make a very fine dish.

G for the *German* you pretended was here,
But he couldn't look real without sausage and beer!
And our *Gramophone*, too, we mustn't forget,
Which cheers us all up when its wintry and wet.

H for the *Haste* when new wounded arrive:
Sort them and name them! Now, then, look alive,
The doctor's here, and your wound's to be dressed—
Time later on for a bath and a rest.
Give up your kit! Hand over your pay!
There isn't a thing that's not taken away!

I for *Incinerator*. Why won't he burn?
Whoever's put in wet leaves from the urn?
Coax him and coddle him—hurry up, run!
Fetch all your scraps, for he's burning like fun!

J for the *Jocks*, wha hail frae the North,
In kilt and Glengarry they braw sally forth.

K for the *Kaiser*. When I came to this letter,
The censor stopped in—well, perhaps, it was better!

L for the *Letters*. So-and-So's got a lot;
I wonder how many best girls he's got?

M is for *Madam*, in royal red,
Our wonderful, splendid, respected head.
M will suggest Dr. *Mason* too—
"Good morning, Sonny, and how are you?"
M is already a fortunate letter,
If we add to it *Mary*, why, none can be better!
Mary, the joke and delight of the place,
With a good-humoured grin on her jolly round face!

N for the *Nurses*, both night and day,
You could'nt have better I hope you'll say!

O for the *Orderlies* rushing about,
Pretending to work, I haven't a doubt!

P for *Potatoes*, for Peel and for Pound,
There are 96 men; will they ever go round?

Q for Q.M., "Oh where can she be?"
"I came here first, a clean towel for me."
"I want eight shirts!" "—" "Which broom may I use?"
"I've broken ten cups!" "—" "I've lost my shoes!"
"The fruit has'nt come!" "—" "The milk's turned sour!"
"And dinner's been waiting about an hour!"

R for the *Rules*, which have to be kept,
You should'nt have sung when you ought to have slept!

S is for *Shorncliffe*. Is Tuesday your day?
Good luck when you leave us. Good-bye! and Hooray!

T for the *Telephone*. Look out, I say!
Here's the Adjutant rushing from far away!

U for your *Uniform*, red, white, and blue,
There are several mixed lots, and some khaki, too.

V for the *Visitor*—excitement to see—
Is it sister or cousin he's got here to tea?

W for *Woodbines* each morning at nine:
"Will you have shag?" "No, mixed's more my line!"

X for *X-ray*. You *must* make a point
Of getting a print of your broken joint.

Y's Dr. *Yolland*, who inspires us with fright.
"Your cap is all crooked, your apron a sight!"

Z for the *Zeal* we all of us show,
In trying to make our own Hospital go!

46. St Anselm's Hospital Alphabet

17.10.1915

I had been told that I was to be discharged from hospital in a few days, and Lady Matthews kindly invited me to dinner with her and her family on Sunday the 17th October.

After dinner we had a walk, returned to tea, and later went back to hospital.

I might mention that Lady Sargant and Lady Matthews were very kind to me and I would be allowed out of hospital, especially to have a game of tennis occasionally with their daughters - a privilege which I was most pleased to accept - and many an afternoon I enjoyed with these girls.

19.10.1915

On Tuesday the 19th October I left hospital at Walmer and, with about 20 others, went to the station to catch the train. As is the custom when a party was leaving hospital, most of the men who could walk came to the station to give those departing a cheer, as it was always understood they were taking their first step towards again returning to France.

We got a good send off and arrived at Shorncliffe Station about 9.30am. We were then met by ambulances and taken up the hill to the very large Canadian hospital there, where we got fresh issues of clothing and leave for 10 days.

On the way up the hill our ambulance had a collision, and we finished the journey with the two front wheels pointing towards one another.

About midday I sent a wire to my sister stating the time of the train I was catching and arrival at London Bridge, where I was met by her.

After a cup of tea at a shop nearby, we caught a train to Balham.

It was rather funny that at Balham Station when we were getting into a taxi for home, I gave the wrong address and was almost ready to argue that the address I mentioned was that of home, but as a matter of fact it was the address of a friend who lives nearby.

I spent the evening at home, very content to think that once more I was within the family circle.

My 10 days' leave was occupied in visiting friends, etc., and, although on the whole I had a very quiet time, it flew rapidly by.

On one day I was taken rather queer and was forced to the conclusion that I had left hospital before I was fit.

29.10.1915

My leave expired on Friday the 29th October, and I reported to the Headquarters of the 3rd Battalion Queen's Westminster Rifles at Richmond, and as instructed reported to the doctor, who, however, ordered me back to hospital.

30.10.1915

As I had brought nothing with me, he extended my pass for another day, so that I could go home and next morning, Saturday the 30th October I went to Richmond and from there was sent to the 2nd London General Hospital, Chelsea (St Mark's College) was ordered to bed and did not get up for nearly a fortnight.

11.11.1915

On Thursday the 11th November, I was getting on pretty well but the doctor in charge thought that I was unlikely to become fit, and I had my papers filled in for discharge from the Army.

12.11.1915

On Friday the 12th November, I was allowed up, and in the afternoon went for a motor drive and tea at a house in the West End.

This I might mention was the first time I had been out with a lady driving the motor car.

We went through St James Park and saw the captured German guns, aeroplane, torpedo and searchlight which were on exhibition there.

15.11.1915

On Monday the 15th November there was a death in the ward in which I was, of an Irish soldier, (Private Walsh), and he was a Catholic.

About six o'clock in the evening the priest administered the last Sacraments, and he asked me to serve, which I readily did.

16.11.1915

On Tuesday the 16th November I went before a medical board and was proposed for discharge. Not feeling as if I would like to get out of the army after having been through a part of the campaign, I asked that I might not be discharged, and was therefore placed on Home Service, which request was acceded to.

After this date I was allowed out several times for motor drives.

20.11.1915

On Saturday the 20th November, I went for a trip through Epsom, Chessington and Surbiton, Sir Albert Stanley and Lady Stanley entertained us to tea. It is interesting in this connection that Sir Albert Stanley has lately taken over the Presidency of the Board of Trade under the Ministry of Mr Lloyd George.

29.11.1915

On Monday the 29th November I was informed that I was to be transferred to the Military Convalescent Hospital, Woodcote Park, Epsom, and at about 10.30am, with two or three others I got into a motor and proceeded on our way.

The driver, however, did not know his way, but I had a fair idea. We were however, by no means anxious to get too quickly to Epsom, so the poor driver was induced to take a route via Wimbledon, Kingston, Hampton Court, Chessington, Leatherhead, and thence to Epsom, having done about twice the actual distance.

In the afternoon I got out of hospital and went home, and on several afternoons I was able to do this.

I was ordered massage treatment, which took up a fair amount of my time, but this did not often interfere with my trips to Streatham.

2.12.1915

On Thursday the 2nd December I had the pleasure of meeting in Epsom a member of the Westminster's Signal Section[55] who was in a hospital nearby, and I managed to get some of the latest news regarding the movements of the dear old "Westminsters".

24.12.1915

As the troops in the hospital were to be entertained by various ladies and certain celebrations were to take place on Christmas Day, an order was issued that no leave was to be given at Christmas time.

On hearing this I awaited my opportunity and seeing the Colonel around the camp, got him and asked if he would allow me to get home for Christmas. He, however, said that it was impossible.

There was therefore no other means open but to take leave, which I accordingly did, and for a very small sum the sergeant in charge of the ward in which I was placed, arranged that he would not mark me absent.

I got home about eight o'clock and sat up until I turned out about 11.30pm to attend Midnight Mass at St Anselm's, Tooting Bec. We got back about 3.00am.

---

[55] Rfm Read.

25.12.1915

On Christmas Day, 25th December, I caught the train over to Sydenham where I was to spend Christmas.

It is interesting to note that not only soldiers absent themselves but also naval officers, which is illustrated by the fact that one of my brothers who was home on leave from the Dardenelles whilst his ship was in port at Naples, was due back yesterday, but he also was with us on Christmas Day.

27.12.1915

We had a very jolly Christmas Day, and Boxing Day, and on Monday the 27th December, my brother proceeded to join his ship at Naples and I went back to hospital, and I was pleased to find there was no trouble regarding my absence.

28.12.1915

The next day, Tuesday the 28th December, the Colonel sent for me, which, by the way put me in great fear, and asked me if I would like to attend a retreat[56] at Isleworth, which I was very pleased to accept.

We got off in charabancs about ten o'clock and arrived at Isleworth about noon.

30.12.1915

The retreat finished on Thursday the 30th December with a visit to Westminster Cathedral and an audience with Cardinal Bourne. After this we had tea on the premises of the Catholic Women's League, and with Father Plater SJ, returned to hospital.

There are no further events that I can call to mind, and the year of 1915 which had been so eventful for me passed away, but the memory of the incidents in the first portion of the year, and the incidents of the latter portion, so happy, will be ever in my memory.

---

[56] The first for soldiers.

47. Retreat House for Men

THE FIRST RETREAT FOR CATHOLIC SOLDIERS.

48. The First Retreat for Catholic Soldiers

Epilogue

I have completed the story of events as far as I am concerned during this Great War which is still bathing Europe in blood.

On the whole, whether serving at home, in training or at the front, I had a very happy time with my regiment.

Although perhaps the more tragic incidents are related and remain in my memory, there are still the very many jolly hours to be accounted for which were spent whilst at the front. There are one or two very outstanding experiences, which I encountered I will always remember.

For instance, crossing the Channel on the way to France; my first entry into the trenches when I was on my own; the long periods in the trenches during the winter; the first time going through Ypres; the battle in which we were involved on the 16/17th June 1915, and above all the battle of Hooge on the 9th August 1915, with all its bloodshed.

The prominent points as regards fun and pleasure whilst around Armentières were: the chimney climbing incident and cycling in the dark under fire which was most exhilarating, the jolly times we had in Houplines and the spontaneous entertainments we used to have in the Chateau.

The chicken incident whilst at Ypres is the one which sticks in my mind, but none of these incidents I am sure will I ever forget.

I might here say a word about the nurses of the Volunteer Aid Detachment Hospitals.

When one takes up the paper it is not often that there is much stated with reference to these girls, who do so much for the soldiers quite voluntarily. The newer members have uncongenial tasks, such as sweeping floors, cleaning, dusting etc., and attending to all manner of men. The more advanced have the dressing of gaping wounds and attending to their disabilities.

A SIGNALLER'S WAR

The nurses at Walmer always had a smiling face and a cheery word for everybody. They were on duty from 7.00am in the morning and often continued until late at night.

They looked after us in every detail in as perfect a manner as possible, and no one can say too much in praise of these splendid workers.

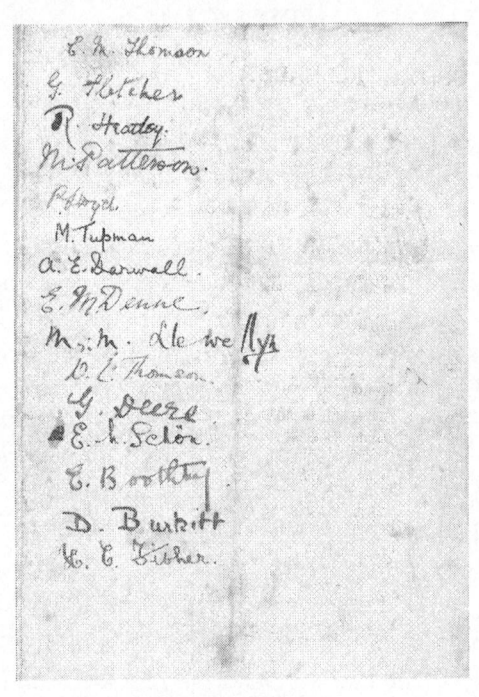

49. Nurses' Signatures

The hospital in which we were had been built as a residence for Sir Charles and Lady Sargant, and when War was declared they resided in a smaller house and gave up this fine building for sick and wounded soldiers.

Sir Charles Sargant is a Justice in the Law Courts.

The grounds attached, which were all at the disposal of the men were very large and permitted such games as golf, bowls, etc.

The house was beautifully clean and furnished most comfortably, and there are a good many men today, who have to thank Lady Sargant for their health, which they recovered through her kindness and attention.

Perhaps it will not to be out of place here to quote a letter received by my mother from Major Cohen, the second in command of the Queen's Westminsters, on my leaving the regiment:

Queen's Westminster Rifles
18.8.1915

Dear Madam,

I am just writing you a line to tell you that your son, Rifleman B.J. Brookes of our signals section, went down to hospital on August 9th, suffering from nerve shock as a result of heavy bombardment on that date. He has not written to us, though no doubt he has to you. I have no doubt from what our doctor tells me, that he will soon begin to get better as the result of rest and absence of bombardment. I should like to let you know that the section all miss him and hope he will soon get well, and I personally regret the loss, even temporarily, of a useful and efficient member of my section.

Yours faithfully,

(signed) J Waley Cohen,
Major

Since the receipt of the above, I have of course, written many times to Major Cohen, as well as to the members of the Signal Section, but I regret to say, that since the 1st July 1916, none of my letters have been answered by my friends, for they are either killed or missing, as I have seen from the letters returned with this marked on them. My best chum Rifleman G.A. Dear, I much regret to say is missing, and I fear that he is dead. (Since confirmed.)

However, I will never regret joining the Army so early in the war, nor my going to France and spending the winter of 1914/1915 in the trenches, although conditions were so bad.

It has a certainly made me take a different view of human nature and life in general, and more than ever appreciate the benefits of HOME.

"The Monthly Tonic"

No. 1.   —.—.—   MARCH, 1918.   —.—.—   Price One Penny.

THE EDITOR "CHATS".

When once the shilling is taken, a Soldier is prepared to run many risks. We on our part have faced the foe without flinching, have shed our blood without a murmur, and have been ready to sacrifice our life if necessary.

Nevertheless, it is with fear and trembling that we have ventured to start this Magazine. Although there is no question about the value of this monthly Tonic, we need the hearty co-operation of all ranks to ensure the success of our future issues. It is chiefly for the patients of this Hospital to have a record of their stay here, that this Magazine has been commenced, and it is the Patients themselves as well as the Staff, from whom we require support in the way of articles, etc. Therefore, please do not forget to send along any matters likely to be of use in the publication of the Magazine. Although it is recognised that there is little room for improvement, we will endeavour to put forward a more attractive Magazine on every publication, and next month we hope to have a Special Article from Surgeon-General F.H. Benson regarding his Indian experiences, and other attractive features.

We desire to thank our Readers for the number of encouraging letters received, including that from Surgeon-General Benson, which is reproduced on Page 10, and to whom we are indebted for the title of this Magazine.

THE EDITOR.

50. The Monthly Tonic

Conclusion

I am still in the Army, and on my discharge from Epsom hospital as a patient, I was taken on the staff, and in gradual steps from Lance Corporal, Corporal, I have risen to the rank of Sergeant, and am in charge of the orderly room at this hospital which contains over 4,500 troops, both British and Colonials.

Whilst doing duty here, I was in attendance on the Commandant, (Colonel Kilkelly, CMG, MVO), when His Majesty the King visited the hospital, and I had the experience, which is by no means to be envied, of walking through the lines of troops behind the King and Colonel Kilkelly during his inspection.

51. King George V with Author in Attendance

I was also with Colonel Kilkelly when Lord Roseberry opened some new tea rooms in the hospital.

Towards the end of August 1915 the Canadian authorities took over the administration of this hospital, with Major L.E.W. Irving, DSO, as Commandant.

As far as I can see, I will be here for "duration of war", but one never knows what will turn up and upset my calculations.

52. The King and Queen Visit Hospitals at Epsom

However, although it may not seem noble, I must say I am quite willing to finish my soldier's career in this campaign, midst the beauties of the country around the famous Epsom Downs, having certainly had enough of active service at the front during the 10 months I spent in Flanders.

_ _ _ FINIS _ _ _

(signed) B J Brookes[57]
Qmsgt

30/6/1918

---

[57] 1st September 1917. Transferred for duty to the Military Convalescent Hospital, Woldingham.
Promoted Company Quarter Master Sergeant.
Promoted Regimental Quarter Master Sergeant (Warrant Officer).

APPENDIX

This timeline shows key dates in the author's war.

4.8.1914	War declared
7.8.1914	Joined Queen's Westminster Rifles
1.11.1914	Departed for France
9.8.1915	Invalided by shell blast
12.8.1915	Transferred to hospital in England
25.10.1915	Engagement to Emmie broken off
16.11.1915	Placed on Home Service
24.2.1916	Promoted to Lance Corporal
17.5.1916	Promoted to Corporal
25.9.1917	Promoted to Company Quarter Master Sergeant
27.11.1917	Promoted to Regimental Quarter Master Sergeant
14.1.1918	Riband for '1914 Star'
20.4.1918	Became engaged to Nora Una Cole
11.11.1918	Peace
14.1.1919	President of Sergeant's Mess
15.5.1919	Married Nora at St Anselm's, Tooting Bec
5.6.1919	Demobbed
7.7.1919	Returned to work at Bunge & Co. @ £3 per week
15.9.1919	Started new job at Société Générale de Paris @ £4 per week

The "Queen's" memorial window was destroyed by blast in 1940. There is now a roll of honour to the Queen's Westminsters in the nave.

53. "Queen's" Memorial Window, Westminster Abbey

"QUEEN'S" ABBEY WINDOW

Prince of Wales Unveils Memorial to Famous London Corps.

The Prince of Wales, who is honorary colonel of the Queen's Westminster Civil Service Rifles yesterday unveiled in Westminster Abbey a window erected to the memory of officers, non-commissioned officers and riflemen of the Queen's Westminsters who fell during the war.

The Abbey was crowded with representatives of the regiment, past and present, relatives of the fallen and a general company.

The window which has been placed in St. Benedict's Chapel, is a very beautiful one. In it are represented the ruins of Ypres Cathedral and the Church of the Holy Sepulchre at Jerusalem, where the regiment rendered notable service.

54. Prince of Wales Unveils Memorial

The author served in the Home Guard during the Second World War. He is seated in the front row, second from the right in this photo.

55. Home Guard 1945

The author and his wife had five children. The elder two served in the forces during the Second World War.

56. Author with Nora and Family, VE day 1945

The next two photos were taken by the author's daughter, Una, on a visit to Sanctuary Wood, which is now a museum where the battlefield has been preserved.

57. Trenches, Sanctuary Wood 2004

58. Shell Holes, Sanctuary Wood 2004

Printed in Great Britain
by Amazon.co.uk, Ltd.,
Marston Gate.